Life in the Fat Lane

Life in the Fat Lane

(My Life as I Lived It)

Phyllis Dianna Tinseth Chi

To order additional copies of this book, contact:
Xlibris Corporation
1-888-795-4274
www.Xlibris.com
Orders@Xlibris.com
61596

Contents

DEDICATION

This book is dedicated to my family. Most have supported and put up with me all these years. And also to friends, students, co-workers, bosses, and subordinates without whom there would be no book. Many will be surprised to find they are in the book and to some I apologize, but if I didn't portray them as they were, there wouldn't be very many lessons in life or humor to share. There is nothing more humorous than real life. Experiences are true as I remember them.

Prologue

Okay, so a lot of people think they have a book inside of them just waiting to pop out. I'm just like a lot of other people. The problem was simply (?) to explore myself and see what kind of book was waiting inside of me. When I first thought about writing, I had no idea that getting a book to pop out would make popping out babies seem like a walk in the park! A mystery thriller crossed my mind, but I realized that as much as I enjoy reading mystery thrillers, I routinely don't figure out "who dunnit" so decided I probably wouldn't be able to conjure up a good thriller—certainly not with a complex plot and character development that would keep the attention of the reader.

I thought about maybe writing a hot passionate paperback that women would read under the hair drier (do women still do that?) or while popping bon bons on the couch. However, my life experiences in this category are deplorable. I married at 29 years of age to the first and last man with whom I would ever share my bed. You may wonder why I waited so long to marry. It is simple; nobody asked me. Those were the days when women didn't ask. I also had truly not found any man with whom I thought I could spend the rest of my life. I had to be careful. My heredity indicated that I would likely live to 80 years of age or more . . . . that is a long time to be married to the same man, especially the wrong man. Divorce isn't in my vocabulary; although I have met some men over the years, who would bring that quickly to my thoughts.

I thought about writing an autobiography but, who in the world would want to read through all those years, and how do you market a book about Phyllis Chi? There is not a lot of name recognition in that one so marketing it would be problematic. I don't think I have a story that would have mass appeal.

As I went through notes of my life that I have kept in a small blue suitcase since I began my professional career as a high school teacher in 1967, I realized that there were some common threads in those notes. First, they were all real life experiences, and second, many of them were funny. That was it; a bathroom or coffee table book with lots of anecdotes, some real lessons in living and something to fit the attention span of the channel surfing, video gaming, cell phoning generation who need something they can pick up, read a few pages and put down again. You won't have to remember what page you are on and can skip around in the book without missing anything—perfect, no plot to develop and no characters to keep track of except me and a few of my closest friends and relatives. And, as I was born in the late 40's there will be some nostalgia in this book for my generation and lots of history of the "way it was" for the younger generation who pick this up and begin to read.

If this book serves only as a record of my life for my children I will be happy. The initial printing will probably be 5 copies in paperback, but you never know whether or not it will appeal to others. If others find it interesting, useful or fun, that is just icing on the cake. So sit back, relax and enjoy.

Chapter 1

When I was Young . . .

(For Those of You Who Thought I Never Was)

Between 1866 and 1876 Scandinavian settlers began to homestead in the western part of Minnesota. More and more farmers came to the area that would be called Scandiaville. Soon some officials of the Northern Pacific Railroad laid out and platted the town. As buildings were added, the town began to take shape. It is believed that in 1882, when a Post Office was built, they had to find a new name because Minnesota already had a town called Scandia. There was a lake south of town called Lake Cyrus so they took that name for the new town. When I came along in 1945 the town hadn't really grown beyond a few hundred people. Everyone in town, with only a handful of exceptions, was either Norwegian or Swedish. Almost everyone was Lutheran . . . with a Swedish Lutheran Church on one end of main street and the Norwegian Lutherans on the other end.

I loved living in Cyrus. I think fondly of the great times and advantages I had because I grew up in Cyrus. When I graduated from high school I think the population was around 350 people. Life in Cyrus was simple, but when I look back on it I realize that we really didn't lack anything of importance.

Living in a farming community, the radio was often turned to 830, WCCO, a Minneapolis station that was then geared to the farmers. It came on very early in the morning, and many farmers listened to it in the wee hours of the morning as they milked the cows in the barn or were doing other chores. There was lots of weather and news and a couple of newscasters named Boone and Erickson who were really full of humor and fun to listen to. One day in the 70's they had a few lines about various conventions that would be held in appropriate cities and towns in Minnesota. i.e. "The Clockmakers Convention will be in Elgin." They asked people to send in more. I took out the Minnesota Atlas to see all the town names in Minnesota, and below is the original list I made up and sent to them. I don't know if they ever read any on the air, but these were my originals at that time.

Minnesota Misspellers	Minneota
Orangutan Society	Gibbon
Chiropractic Association	Aitkin
Society of Knitters	Angora
Butchers	Angus
American Indian Movement	Apache
Ding Dongs	Avon
Circus Performers	Barnum
Pie Makers, Inc.	Barry
Veterans	Battle Lake
National Audubon Society	Bird Island
Rolaids International	Borup
Baking Powder Producers	Calumet
Soup Makers	Campbell
Dept. of Natural Resources	Clearbrook
Honeymooners, Int'l.	Climax
Perfume Makers	Cologne
Chefs of America	Cook
Christmas Tree Growers	Pine City
Evolutionists	Darwin
Nudists	Embarrass
Organ Manufacturers	Hammond
Barbershop Quartets	Harmony
Dolly Parton Fan Club	Hill City
Orientals	Rice

River Boat Captains	Jordan
Car Manufacturers	Sedan
Pen Manufacturers	Shafer
Shriners Post-Conv. Seminar	Sleepy Eye
Office Supply Equip. Co.	Staples
Highway Patrolmen	Traffic
Tree Growers of America	Twig
Typewriter Manufacturers	Underwood
Norwegians	Viking
Polacks	Warsaw

Another popular radio station with teenagers was KDWB, Channel 63. And, being in the High School class of 1963, we stole their slogan, "63, that's easy to remember" as an unofficial class motto. This station was the rock 'n roll station, and we listened to it a lot. WCCO was for the old folks, and KDWB was for the young ones. There was also a radio station in Morris, a town about 10 miles away, which was more local. The other two were out of the Twin Cities.

There were two popular newspapers throughout Minnesota in those days. The Minneapolis Tribune was a morning paper, and the Minneapolis Star was an evening paper. I don't recall if we got the daily papers, but we did get the Sunday newspaper. Each Sunday, when I was young, there was a crossword puzzle called Prizeword Pete. It was the size of a postcard, and people were encouraged to do the puzzle, cut it out, paste it on a postcard and mail it in for prizes. My Grandma Felt did the puzzle faithfully every week, and I remember working on it with her. She mailed it in frequently but never did get a prize. It was fun solving the puzzle with her. She and my mom always loved doing crossword puzzles.

In those days almost everybody had a drawer or box in their kitchen for savings stamps. There were green stamps and Gold Bond stamps. You would get stamps based on the amount of purchases at certain stores. There were small books to paste the stamps in, and when you got full books of stamps, you could turn them in for free gifts. There were other stamps too, that were only for certain stores. I just remember the drawer stuffed with stamps and books, and it was always a mess.

We had a creamery in our town where they made butter and of course produced milk and cream. They also had storage lockers that people rented for frozen meat. I remember it was fun to go "down to the creamery" to get packages of roasts or steaks or hamburger out of our locker. It was a neat place, and I remember I liked the smell. Probably ice cream. Later we got a deep freeze in our basement, so we no longer rented a locker at the creamery. The creamery was on the other side of downtown so about 4 blocks from our house that was on the other edge of town.

While I attended school, all 12 years in the same building, we lived a half block from the school. My dad built two small story and a half houses next to each other. Then he helped my Grandpa and Grandma Felt (mom's parents) sell their small dairy farm near Itasca Park and moved them into one of the houses and us into the other. Mom's parents were very poor, and the farm was not very valuable so to help them prepare for old age my Dad hired Grandpa Felt to work for him in the garage he owned in Cyrus. He did this so he could pay into social security for Grandpa thus assuring him of some income to live on when he would no longer be able to work. When they left the farm and moved to Cyrus, it became home base to their four sons too—Lloyd, Norris, Mervin and Orville. Mervin and Orville were still living at home so they moved too. Three of mom's brothers married Cyrus girls. Mervin married Donna Larson; Orville married Lorraine Barsness; and Norris married Elaine Mickelson. Mervin eventually bought out the gas station from dad and ran it for years before moving to Glenwood. Orv went to Minnesota School of Business and never lived in Cyrus. He started out working for Robin Hood then later International MultiFoods. Their family lived in Detroit, Venezuela and Mexico before moving back to Burnsville.

Norris and Elaine moved to California after they married. I was a flower girl at their wedding. When they celebrated their 50th anniversary, I mailed my flower girl dress to them as a gift. Mom's oldest brother, Lloyd, is the only one who married a girl from outside of Cyrus. He met his wife when he was hospitalized while stationed in the Navy in California. I think his wife, Jean, was a volunteer at the hospital, and that is where they met. She was a native Californian. They live in California, and he did auto body work until he retired.

Dad was born and raised in Cyrus. His mother passed away when he was around 11 years old, so he and two sisters, Doris and Ruby, were left with their dad. Their dad later remarried to Magna, and they had one daughter, Lorraine. Ruby married Harold Wolters, moved to Iowa, and still lives there; Doris lived in Minneapolis; and Lorraine moved to Mayville, North Dakota, where she and her husband Kenneth Eken still live. None of dad's sisters married men from Cyrus. Doris passed away a few years ago. She had been married twice. First, to Gilbert Christensen and later to Marvin Johnson.

Dad was the oldest child in his family and had all sisters. Mom was the oldest child in her family and had all brothers. They married, and had all daughters, so there are no Tinseth's to carry on the Tinseth name for his branch of the Tinseth Family tree.

Garage sales were popular back in those days too. One of the first big ones mom had was a lot of fun. Grandma Felt helped with the sale. There was always a big board to put tags on, and the tags always had the initials of whose item it was, so at the end of the day everyone who participated could divide up the profits. Dad gave mom and Grandma carpenter aprons with pockets to wear to keep the money in. Then during the sale he would slip extra dollars into Grandma's apron and slip extra tags on the board with mom's initials. He did this for years, and Grandma and he shared this secret. When my sister Kathy moved to Hinckley, we would have family rummage sales up there, and dad padded the money and the tags there too. After the first few sales and mom bragging to all her friends about how much money she always made, dad decided that he could never tell her about his little "donations." So we have all kept this secret all these years. She did have some great sales, but never as good as she thought!!

Another event that I haven't heard of for years is the Box Social. It was sponsored by the Luther League (young folks group at Church). Each girl and woman would prepare a box lunch with sandwiches, cakes or pies, and lots of homemade goodies. Then they would decorate their boxes with paper and flowers or ribbons and bows. The next step was to sneak the boxes into the Church basement, so nobody would know who made which box. Then, after an evening of fun and games, the boxes would be auctioned off as a kind of fund raiser. Each box was then shared for lunch by the person who brought it and the boy or man who bought it.

Another Social was the Ice Cream Social. This was also a big event. They were usually held on someone's farm. Tables and chairs were set up outside on a beautiful summer evening, and pie and ice cream was served. I recall sometimes they were held in the church basements.

Every event at our school always brought a crowd. For example, everybody went to the basketball games. The gym was not huge. There was room for two rows of folding chairs on each side of the gym. One end was the entry and ticket booth, and the other end had the stage that was used for plays and concerts. There were also balconies along both sides of the gym—each wide enough for two rows of bleacher-style seating. During one basketball game a lady was leaning over the railing yelling at the team, and her false teeth fell out and landed on the gym floor beneath. To many this gym probably reminded them of an elevator with no "Up" button. To me it seemed huge. The school was so small that when the band played the National Anthem or played some music during half time, the basketball players had to hop up on the stage and join us, or we wouldn't have all of the instruments necessary for the songs.

I only had one trip to the principal's office for disciplinary reasons all during high school. It was a result of halftime music at a basketball game. Our director said we were going to play a particular song, and I was the only trumpet player who showed up that particular night. There was a trumpet part in the middle of the song that was only trumpets and some drums. At the time I was 2nd chair trumpet, so I didn't even play the melody during the trumpet part. I raised my hand and told the director that we couldn't play that song because there would be no melody, etc. He said that didn't matter. Rather than make a fool of myself, I decided to make him the fool. When we got to the middle trumpet part, I left my trumpet in my lap, and he fanned his arms in the air with no trumpet being played, just two drummers. He was pretty irritated. The next morning when I showed up for band practice 1st hour he said I was wanted in the principals' office. When I got in the office, the principal closed his door and asked me what happened at halftime the night before. I told him the story, and he said, "I thought the song had a weird part in the middle. That explains it." He said to just go back to band and not to do it again. Then he smiled and winked.

The gym was also used annually for the school carnival. Men in the community would build booths along the sides of the gym for ring toss and other carnival games. The women would put on a cake walk on the stage. There were refreshments in the cafeteria. There were always crowds of people and lots of fun. I remember buying little bags of confetti to throw around and winning little trinkets as prizes and treasuring them.

In 1961, when I was in my sophomore year of high school some of us wrote letters to Norway to become pen pals with Norwegian boys. We were boy crazy I suppose. In March I received an Air Mail letter from Tor H. Ronning, Slettas pr. Rena, Norway. I'll never forget the excitement when I received his letter. Everyone gathered around to read it. He wrote from a whaling boat somewhere. I sent a letter back, immediately planning a trip to Norway to meet him when I got out of high school. But, I never heard from him again. And I've never been to Norway either. I'll never know if he made it home from the sea or simply decided not to bother being a pen pal with a farm girl from America. Here is his letter:

Dear Phyllis,

I got your name from a friend of mine, John. He can not write or speak English, therefor he came to me and asked me to translate your letter knowing I could speak English.

Neither I have ever had a pen pal. Therefor I made up my mind to write to you. As I am not an Englishman, I think you will find many a mistake in this letter. But I hope you understand mostly of it, and send me an answer.

I am tall, 1 m 82 cm, have dark blond hear, blue eyes, and I am 17 years old. Both mother and father are full-blooded Norwegians. I have a sister at 8 years, and a brother at 16. We live in a little village named Slettas. It has the population of about 300.

When this letter is written I am in the South-Atlantic ocean fishing whale. It is not too amusing but, it is a good place to be if you want to save money, because here it is no chance at all to spend it.

I am interested in all kinds of sports. I enjoy music too and to read books is my greatest pleasure.

Pleas, do me the favour and answer this letter. If you do not want to do it, ask some of your girl friends to write to me.

Sincerely,
Tor and John

P.S. If you make up your mind for write, do not use South Georgia address on this letter, but send to Norway because I will be home in 2 months.

We had scandal in our town too. A previous band director was found in a remote area outside of town in a car making out with a high school girl. The wife of a businessman was a kleptomaniac, and her husband just told store owners to watch her and keep track, and he would pay them for whatever she took. One pastor that was in town for a short time was suspected of being a window peeper. There were rumors of affairs, but most were never substantiated. In a town that small I don't know how anybody thought they could get by with anything without being seen by somebody.

We also had our share of girls getting pregnant and most of them getting married. A single pregnant girl was not accepted in school like now. One classmate who got pregnant came into the school after the regular school day for her classes because she was not allowed to attend regular classes in her condition. Another girl got pregnant, and so they set a date for their wedding. The girls in our class decided to give her a bridal shower. One day a couple of us were in the Red Owl Store buying stuff for the shower when the pregnant girl's father came in and said, "The wedding is off. She lost the baby." Then he walked out and left us in stunned silence. I don't know if they ever married. In those days, in that small town, getting married if the girl was pregnant was the thing to do, whether right or wrong. I'm sure there were many marriages that ended up great, but there were also some that probably should have never happened.

People who were invited to a wedding sat in the sanctuary. Those that weren't invited but wanted to see the wedding were welcome to sit in the balcony of the church and simply observe. A couple of the ladies in town were regulars, and we always joked that they probably went home and marked their calendars to see how many months from the wedding until the first baby!

We had one wedding in our church where a girl's previous boyfriend threatened to come to the church and disrupt the ceremony. Nothing happened, but my dad and a few others were sitting in the back pews keeping an eye out in case he showed up.

Most weddings were followed by a reception in the church basement, at least in our Lutheran Church. There was usually a buffet of sandwiches and salads and then cake. At weddings and funerals 'church meat' sandwiches were often served. They consisted of ground ham and hard cooked eggs, mixed with mayo and pickle relish and spread on buns. Funerals always had jello, salad, sandwiches, and cake. The most wonderful smell, though, was always the coffee. The huge black coffee pots cooking on the massive stoves in the kitchen were for 'egg coffee.' I don't know what eggs did to the coffee, but eggs were mixed with the grounds, and everyone raved about the coffee and always bragged when it was 'egg coffee.' I wonder if anybody still makes 'egg coffee.'

Funerals were not something children usually attended. They were often held while we were at school. Sometime during the funeral, maybe at the end, the church bell would ring indicating the years of age of the deceased. The saddest day was the very few rings for a classmate's little brother who had been killed in a gun accident. I felt sorry for the bell ringer when someone in their 90's passed. I just remember we would sit in school and silently count the rings.

Sunday morning church had its rituals. There was no coffee after services. We all went home because most moms had something baking in the oven to be ready when we got home. Often mom would be searing a roast on top of the stove early Sunday morning. She would get a pan very hot and quickly brown the top and bottom of the roast before putting it in the oven to bake while we were in church. Sometimes she would put chicken in the oven. I just know that the wonderful odors that greeted us when we walked in the door of our house after church are never forgotten.

Eva played the organ at our church, and Gordon was the pianist for the choir and her backup organist. Eva taught elementary school and also gave piano lessons in her home. She was married to a man who often did not attend church and appeared to be drunk a lot. Eva didn't have a sense of smell. Rumors in town were that she never even knew her husband drank because she couldn't smell it or didn't admit it. Sometimes he would be falling down drunk, and she thought he had a bad back. She taught my dad in elementary school and then me. She lived to be 100 and taught generations of Cyrus kids. We used to peak into her classroom after school and giggle as we watched her pick hairs off her chin. I don't giggle now as I do the same thing!

Although Eva taught piano lessons, mom and dad took us kids to Morris to take piano from Mrs. Killoran. I never knew why, or I don't remember. Anyway, my sister Karen became a very good pianist, I am mediocre and my other sister Kathy doesn't play a lot but actually gave piano lessons for awhile. Mrs. Killoran had an organ at one end of her living room and a piano at the other. Every possible surface in her home was piled with music books and sheet music. This included her dining room. The table had piles of music and every chair did too. Somehow she seemed to know which music was in which pile because she would be able to find stuff so easily. She had some sort of system to it. I don't know where they ever sat and relaxed or ate their meals. I never saw the kitchen, so maybe there wasn't any music in that room, but who knows. Their yard and garage looked like a junkyard. The garage was so full of junk that they never pulled a car in. But she was a nice lady and a wonderful teacher.

We had a high school home ec teacher who we thought was as old as the hills. She wore her hair in a pug in the back. One time during a demonstration, where she was seated at the sewing machine and we crowded around her to see her technique, one of the girls dropped sewing pins into her pug. She was very fussy and about drove us nuts, but we learned a lot. I remember we had a foreign foods unit in our cooking class, and we made booklets about the country and included the recipes. I remember actually enjoying her class a lot. To teach us how to upholster furniture, she had us redecorate the teacher's lounge. We painted, made new curtains, reupholstered the sectional sofa and really learned a lot. One time we were required to make a dress with a full length zipper in the back. I remember carefully following her directions and doing my best. When I finished, I removed the basting stitches, used to hold it all together while you sewed the actual seams, only to find that I had the 24" zipper in upside down!!! I never fixed the zipper, and I never wore the dress. I remember it was brown and pretty ugly anyway.

Miss Lewis and Miss Scheffler were two high school teachers who influenced me the most. They were business teachers while I was in high school. I loved the business classes, and they were both wonderful teachers. They both inspired me, and when I decided to major in high school business education at Augsburg, they were women I felt had been true role models as to what kind of teacher I wanted to be.

My older sister wanted to be a band teacher when she went to college. The high school principal, who doubled as guidance counselor, told her that she needed to choose another profession because that was a "man's job." This was in the 60's. So, she went to Augsburg and became a Home Economics teacher; a career she followed for many years. Later, she went into corporate food service in the Twin Cities with Ebenezer Nursing Home and Ridges Nursing Home, then became Director of Food Services at Walker Methodist Health Center and then on to work in facilities for the elderly in the Chicago area. My younger sister became a music teacher, but vocal, not instrumental. When she graduated from Augsburg she went to Hinckley, Minnesota where she taught vocal music for many years. We traveled there many times to attend concerts or musicals that she directed. Unfortunately, her career was cut short when she was forced to retire after being diagnosed with MS.

When I was growing up, Monday was wash day. NO MATTER WHAT! Washing machines were all ringer-style when I was young. You had a washer that agitated the clothes. Then you would put each piece of wash through the wringer (run by a hand crank) to squeeze out the water. The other side of the wringer would drop the clothes into a huge wash tub where mom would swish them in the clear water to get out the soap. Then she would rotate the wringer over by the wash tub and wring them again into a second tub of rinse water that she would swish by hand. Then she would wring them a final time and put them in the basket for carrying outside to hang. The same water was used for each load. Mom started with the cleanest and whitest clothes and worked her way to the final load which was always dad's work clothes because they were the dirtiest. Water was probably cheap, but nevertheless the same wash and rinse water was used over and over. This was also the practice on Saturday night with baths. We did not run fresh bath water for each bath. We took turns, cleanest to dirtiest. And, we often added hot water as the tub cooled off. I can't even imagine anybody does this nowadays, but I think many did it back then.

Once washing machines were outfitted with electric wringers, there would occasionally be a woman with her arm black and blue up to her elbow because she had caught her hand while putting something in the wringer and couldn't stop it quickly enough to avoid injury. This is probably where the phrase used when somebody is in trouble came from . . . "got her tit caught in the wringer." Could be. That would be problematic. If I recall correctly, mom got an automatic washing machine and a dryer when I was in high school.

Mom would be up hours before we left for school, and we would have to hang clothes out for her before we left in the morning. In the winter I remember her bringing in clothes from the line that had frozen dry and were stiff as a board. They were literally freeze dried! Pretty funny. There were no wash and wear fabrics when I was young. Mom put these metal forms inside the legs of dad's pants which helped pull out the wrinkles while they dried. Otherwise EVERYTHING had to be ironed. Mom kept up with the ironing, with our help as we got older. Our neighbor, Mae, had more kids and had trouble keeping up with her ironing. She would sprinkle her clothes, as mom did, and roll them up to distribute the dampness evenly. What she didn't finish ironing she would put in her freezer. I suppose this was so they wouldn't mold if she didn't get them ironed soon? There were no steam irons either, so if something was dry and needed to be ironed right away you would use a sprinkling bottle (like a pop bottle with a special cap on it with holes in it), just sprinkle with their finger tips dipped in water, or use a wet pressing cloth.

One morning my mom heard her mom, my Grandma Felt, laughing out at the clothesline in the backyard. Mom went out to see what was going on, and Grandma had white streaks of bird poop all over her forehead and down her glasses. When she saw mom she said, "They sing for some people!!" They laughed till tears rolled and told the story often.

Our small town had an elderly doctor, so most people went to Morris, Starbuck or Hancock for medical care. Our doctor was in Hancock. I remember a couple of times when he made a house call. It was always for dad, so maybe he made the house call because it was hard for mom to bring dad to his office? I don't really know, but I remember the few house calls and that they were very special and kinda scary. I hated going to the doctor and was terrified of shots. One time he said I had to have a penicillin shot in my butt. I tightened my butt so severely when he put the needle in that it broke. I bet he hated it as much as I did whenever I needed shots.

In the early 50's polio was hitting many families in our town. I remember one night when an ambulance came next door and took by neighbor friend, Spencer, to the hospital because he had polio. The summer when the epidemic was at its worst, everyone was encouraged to stay home and away from crowds. That is the one year we didn't go to the State Fair. That was also the year dad built a wooden playhouse with windows and a front porch, so we would stay in our yard and play. Sometimes we pretended it was our house, and we'd have our dolls in there. Other times it would be a grocery store, and we'd use empty food boxes and cans to fill our shelves. Once in awhile we turned it into a drive-in, and people would walk up to the window and order lemonade. It was a great place to play. Years later, when relatives of neighbors Cliff and Mae lost everything in a fire in a nearby town, dad gave the playhouse to them for their small children. We were in high school by then so didn't mind parting with it. Many years later, dad built another playhouse in our backyard for our sons Jon and Erick. We kept it and moved it with us until we moved off 70th Street in Edina and left it in the backyard.

When we visited dad's sister in Iowa, he would buy a case of oleo with coloring. In our area it was not something people admitted to having in their kitchens. At that time colored oleo was something you couldn't buy in Minnesota. The pound of oleo was in a bag (like a clear chocolate chip size bag) with a yellow/red bubble of dye in the middle. You had to break the bubble within the bag and squeeze the bag to distribute the dye evenly. Oleo bought in Minnesota had no dye so looked more like lard than butter. When mom served this oleo, she always scooped it with an ice cream scoop and put it in a pretty dish. I wonder if she really thought nobody could tell it wasn't real butter? She continued to do that as long as I can remember, whether it was oleo or butter, didn't matter. Most of the time butter was served in a scoop like ice cream.

Speaking of ice cream . . . . Ice cream was a routine evening snack. We would have ice cream, popcorn, cereal or cream and bread before bedtime. I don't think we ever went to bed without a snack. This snack had nothing to do with being hungry. Any wonder we all were pretty robust!

On Sunday nights we would usually have a sandwich because our big meal on Sunday was at noon. Dinner was at noon and supper was in the evening. When we moved to Minneapolis, we got into the habit of calling the evening meal dinner. After we were married, an old college roommate Linda and her husband Darren invited us down to their farm near Zumbrota for dinner one Sunday. We showed up in the late afternoon for dinner. They had eaten and wondered where we were when we didn't show up at noon for dinner. It goes to show you that you don't need to speak different languages to fail to communicate.

Speaking of language, when I was little I could never remember the word vanilla. I just wanted plain white ice cream so I would ask for white ice cream. In those days there was an ice cream called White House. It had cherries and nuts in it. I hated ice cream with cherries and nuts and often got this when I went to Toby's Cafe by myself to get an ice cream cone. I had to spit out all the cherries and nuts and then enjoyed the 'white' ice cream that was left.

Toby's Cafe was a great little place. We would all crowd in there after school events. That's where we discovered that you could put M & M's in a coke bottle, shake it good and hit the ceiling with the fizz. I was on a tug-of-war team once, and the winning team got steak dinners at Toby's. I was on the winning team. I remember that for a little while one summer in high school I got to work a few days at the cafe. I had dreams of taking orders and 'slinging hash.' My job, however, was to be elbow deep in dishwater, not a glamorous job at all. I still remember being very excited to have a job, even though it was very short. Most kids didn't work because there just weren't jobs available for us. I often wondered if my dad convinced Toby to hire me to "get it out of my system."

In the fall the smell of burning leaves was everywhere. We would rake our leaves out to the side of the street in front of our houses and burn them right there. Nobody bagged leaves or hauled them away. We burned them. Sometimes we even roasted marshmallows in the fires. It was fun to play with the fires by putting the rake or a stick in and stirring up the coals when they started to smolder. This would bring up the leaves from underneath, and we would have new flames to play with. I remember liking that smell.

There was no lake in Cyrus, just a creek running near the edge of town. We still took swimming lessons every summer. We went by school bus to Starbuck and took lessons in Lake Minnewaska. An occasional snake slithered through the water and once in awhile there would be a leech/blood sucker between our toes, but we had a great time. Cyrus only had grocery stores, cafes, pool halls, creamery, grain elevator, hardware store, a blacksmith, a post office and a couple of other small businesses. For everything else we had to go to another town. To bowl we usually went to Starbuck. We had to go elsewhere to skate, which we did often. Many times school buses were used to transport kids who were too young to drive. We roller skated in Benson and at the rink called Perkins, near Morris. There was a movie theater in Morris. There was also a drive-in theater in Morris. Morris was the big city. It had a drive-in restaurant, and when I was in high school they opened a branch of the University of Minnesota there. Morris had clothing stores and a drugstore, dentists and beauty shops. At the shoe store in Morris we used to step on an x-ray machine and look at the bones in our feet. Nobody thought anything of it. Morris had a bakery and a hospital. They even had a motel or two.

Cyrus had two small grocery stores. They used to wrap the sanitary napkins boxes in butcher paper and put them back on the shelves. Like nobody knew what they were? We used to buy groceries all month, and then dad would go in and pay the bill. Most of the time the grocer would throw in a piece of candy for us kids at no charge. I remember what a treat it was to have mom buy cookies at the store. We usually only got homemade ones!!

My mom and her friends used to do lots of canning each fall. Mom canned lots of pickles and vegetables and fruit. We always had a garden, and I remember picking green beans and swatting the mosquitoes many times. It was a big deal when the ladies got together for them to brag about how many jars they had "put up" recently. The jars had to be sterilized in huge pots on the stove, then the jars were filled, covers put on and they were lined up on the kitchen cupboard awaiting the "pop" that occurred when they cooled enough to make the lids seal. You would listen for the "pops", and any jars that didn't pop were refrigerated and used right away because they would be poisonous otherwise.

I remember the most fun was canning peaches. Mom would get a kettle boiling full of water. Then she would drop in the whole peach for just a few minutes. Then she would put the peaches into ice water in the sink, and the skin would slip off easily. It was fun to slide the peels off. (This same method was used to slip the skins off beets before canning beet pickles) When she cut the peaches in half and removed the pits, she would arrange the halves in the jars so they were all with the cut side down. Once she had them perfectly arranged she would pour hot sugar syrup over them and put on the lids. They really looked beautiful.

After we got a deep freeze, mom started freezing vegetables, and I remember sitting outside and cutting corn off the cob after the cobs had been blanched (boiled briefly). That is one messy job—best suited to being done outside.

When I was first on my own and before I got married, I did canning, but mostly pickles just because they were so much better than the ones in the stores. A co-worker at the INS, Jeanne, did lots of canning. She used to can meat, potatoes, tomatoes and other things. She often shared them with friends. There are many people who still do canning, but I'm not one of them.

I'm old enough to remember when we began using zip codes. They first started being used in the early 60's. Prior to that cities had a number after the city name, before the state, that indicated the zone. There was no house-to-house delivery in our town. Everybody in town had to go to the post office and check their combination lock box. We had box #94. There was rural delivery.

Two new states were added to the USA when I was in school. First was Alaska in January of 1959 and second was Hawaii in August of the same year. So our flag went from 48 to 50 stars that year. I remember it was exciting when the new flag came out. The rows of stars had to be staggered because 50 wasn't a number that worked—couldn't have 5 rows of 10. To achieve a nice distribution of the 50 five-pointed stars, they ended up with nine offset horizontal rows with six stars in each and alternating them with rows of five stars each. There are rumors on the Internet that a design with 51 stars is already drafted as there are still other possible US Territories that could some day become states. I was 14 when these two states were added, and I remember it was very exciting.

An event in 1954 also sticks in my memory. That was the year "under God" was added to the Pledge of Allegiance. I remember that we had to practice the Pledge to get it right. We said the Pledge of Allegiance every morning in elementary school and I was nine when the words were added. Now there are those who want to take it back out. Whether it is in there or not, we are all "under God."

We didn't have seat belts in cars when I was little, nor did we have special car seats for kids. We often laid above the back seat in the window or on the floor in the back seat and read comic books or played word games. Babies were held in mom's laps. We used to love to ride in the back of the open pickup or the back of the station wagon, rolling around and playing as we went down the road.

People threw stuff out of the car windows without a thought. Everyone used cloth diapers back then and one time dad told of a lady in a car in front of them who shook her baby's diaper out the car window to empty the solid stuff, and it landed on dad's windshield!! I remember throwing gum wrappers or candy wrappers out the car windows. Nobody every told me it was wrong. I wonder why we even thought it was ok?

We never locked our doors when I was a kid. In fact, I remember when mom and dad sold our house in Cyrus and moved to Willmar in the 60's they didn't have any keys to give to the new owners. I don't know if anybody locked their doors but am guessing most did not. As kids I don't recall that we had any fear of being abducted or molested. We ran and played all over town, and our parents didn't have the worries that we have now. It was truly a simple and carefree time.

Chapter 2

South of the Border

(A Summer Vacation in Mexico)

On June 19, 1968 my two sisters and I hopped in my Ford Galaxy 500 and headed South with a final destination of Mexico City. Our mom's brother Orv and his wife and kids lived there after having spent some years in Venezuela with his company. What a great opportunity for us to travel to Mexico. Karen and I were single teachers with our summer free, and our younger sister Kathy was in high school.

We stopped in Dallas en route to San Antonio, so we could see the place where President Kennedy was assassinated in 1963. It was a sobering experience. Our next destination was San Antonio. Once in San Antonio we stayed with an old family friend, Lloyd Dosdall, and his wife Mary Lou. They showed us around San Antonio, mainly the venue that was built for the HemisFair '68. It was the first officially designated World's Fair (or international exposition) held in the southwestern United States. It was held from April 6 through October 6, 1968. As terrified of heights as I am, we all went to the top of the Space Needle (aka: The Tower of the Americas). I stayed close to the center by the elevator when we got to the top. I was doing fine until we read the plaque near the elevator. It stated that the poured concrete core of the

Space Needle wouldn't completely dry for 40+ years! That did not offer me much comfort. It should be dry in a few more years! I was glad to descend in the elevator and arrive alive on the ground!! On a college band tour I had been in the Seattle Space Needle and about kissed the ground when I got down safely. I didn't want to go up in either space needle but figured I'd kick myself later if I did not take the opportunity to do so at the time.

We left our car in the Dosdall's garage, and they took us to the airport for the final leg of our journey to Mexico City. It was aboard a Braniff International Boeing 707 and was pretty exciting. I don't like flying in the clouds as its too much like fog and feels as if we'll hit something. I didn't mind flying above them, though. The clouds were beautiful and looked like huge mountains. At one time during the flight we supposedly saw the Gulf of Mexico. I was disoriented, I guess, 'cause I thought it was just more blue sky. Back then meals on airplanes were better than now. We had shish-kabobs. I was so impressed. That was pretty exotic food for a country girl. My two sisters didn't exactly enjoy flying. Kathy couldn't eat a thing, and we just hoped she'd keep down whatever food she had eaten before the flight. We were in the air an hour and forty minutes. It was really a smooth ride except I thought the landing could have been better . . . kinda felt like the pilot was practicing. When we landed, it was very clear, so we could see all of Mexico City. I think today the smog in Mexico City would make a perfectly clear day a rare occurrence, but I haven't been back since 1968, so I have no personal knowledge of it. I remember some people pointing out landmarks, like the copper dome of the Olympics basketball and sports stadium.

When we were coming down the steps off the plane, a photographer snapped our picture. I was sure he had mistaken me for a movie star but later learned they take everybody's picture. After we got in the car, they came running with the picture to sell it to us—"anything for a peso."

Going through Customs was nothing. Our suitcases were not opened. They didn't much care what we brought into the country. Orv, Lorraine and their youngest child at the time, Richard, met us at the plane. He was 3 years old, so the only one of their kids not in school that day. Their youngest child, Rachel, had not been born yet.

It was hard to believe we were actually in Mexico City. As kids we had crossed the border to Canada on a family trip, but Canada looked like the US, and everybody spoke English. Mexico was really foreign. It looked different. The people looked different. English was not the first language. It was pretty exciting.

Lorraine took us on a road trip of Mexico City the next day. We saw Chapultepec Park, which is the largest park in Mexico. It includes an amusement park which, at that time, had the largest roller coaster in the world, called Russian Mountain. In the Park there was a Rain God made of stone, which was moved to the museum during the dry season. Ironically, legend said it rained the whole day they were transporting it.

The next day Aunt Lorraine took us shopping. We went to two huge department stores, much like Dayton's or Donaldson's in Minneapolis. Shoplifting was openly watched more carefully than I was used to. We had to check our packages when we entered the store, and store guards were plentiful. Two important Spanish words I learned in the store were 'Damas' and 'Caballeros' which were important so you go into the correct restroom. The only foreign language I knew was a bit of Norwegian.

Driving around Mexico City, it was fun to observe traffic circles and the road signs. Many of their signs are more universally understandable with more symbols than are used in the US. Estacionamiento means 'parking'. A no parking zone, for example, is a large sign with an E on it with an X over the E. The traffic was wild compared to Minnesota. I was glad I never drove while we were there. I think I would have been terrified. I had been caught up in a traffic circle in Waco, Texas, on our drive to San Antonio. I think we went around two or three times before we figured out where and how to get off the darn thing!

We went with Aunt Lorraine to register her daughter Denise in the American School. It was a school of about 2,000 students; 40% American, 40% Mexican and 20% from various other countries. Up until 1968 Barb, Beverly and Denise, Orv and Lorraine's other kids, had been attending the Pan American Workshop. This school was started by Bonita Clark Wickson and half of the classes were in English and the rest were in Spanish. It was strictly an academic school—no physical education, no music, etc. The American School more closely resembles a school in the US with the exception of the dual courses in English and Spanish. The American School was a Mexican Educational Institution, thus satisfying Mexico's school requirements. It also had physical education, music, home economics, and best of all, to me as a business teacher, it had a business department in the high school. While there I bought a raffle ticket for the 4th of July celebration that was going to be held on June 29 on the American School Campus.

After leaving the American School we went on a ride around Lomas. It is an old, elegant part of town where many American's lived. We also saw where the US Ambassador lived. We often drove on the Periferico, like Highway 100 in the Twin Cities. There were many fountains and statues. One statue was the Golden Angel, perched atop a tall monument. During an earthquake in 1957 she fell and had later been repaired and returned to the monument. There was also a huge nude statue of the Goddess of the Hunt. At one time, the Decency Society of Mexico had her partially clothed, but when she was taken down to be cleaned for the Olympics, she went back up, once again nude.

One of the first evenings at Uncle Orv's house their housemaid, Maria, made us a Mexican supper consisting of rice, re-fried beans and quesadillas (lefse with meat in it). I recall being glad I was Norwegian and didn't have to eat that stuff all the time. Now I enjoy going to a good Mexican restaurant now and then, but it is still not my favorite ethnic food.

We didn't tour every day. Sometimes we spent the day at home. We often played the game Password. One evening we even made an attempt to learn how to play bridge. It required way too much concentration, and I've never played it since then. Karen is the best seamstress among us, so one day she sewed curtains for Maria and Eva's rooms. They were native Mexican women who lived in during the week. They helped in the household and with the kids. Another local man came once a week, I think, and took care of the indoor garden and the yard. Sometimes we would watch a late movie on TV in English (with Spanish subtitles). Uncle Orv was usually chief in charge of popcorn.

On Sunday, June 23, we all went to church at the Lutheran Church of the Good Shepherd. It was a church that was started in 1963, when two English-speaking parishes of Mexico City merged. They had resulted from mission work on the part of the American Lutheran Church and the Lutheran Church—Missouri Synod. It was not a member of any stateside synodical body, but a wonderful Parish with all of the activities you would find at any Lutheran Church in the US. They held services in English and in Spanish. It had rained every day since our arrival, but the rain stopped long enough so we participated in the coffee hour that was traditionally held on the front lawn of the Church after services. After Sunday dinner, we took a tour of the University of Mexico (Universidad Nacional de Mexico) where many Olympic events were held.

Uncle Orv and his family lived in a part of Mexico City called Pedregal. The homes were beautiful and to me their home was a mansion. It had huge glass windows all along the front and side walls of the main living area. Just closing all the drapes in the evening was a major task. There was a free-standing fireplace in the middle of the living room. What I liked the best was the huge bathtub in the master bedroom. I don't remember if it was round or square, just big!! The kids loved to all get in and play in that tub, and I suppose they got clean besides.

Just outside Pedregal were acres of shacks, literally made of cardboard and tar paper where many lower class Mexican's lived. The area looked filthy, crowded, and really a sad sight. However, the people themselves were amazingly clean. Women could be seen sweeping the dirt in front of their shelters, and the children playing in the streets often wore sparkling white clothes.

Pedregal itself is a huge lava bed covered with ultra-modern elegant homes. The pools, gardens and homes are spectacular. All of the homes are walled in—some with beautiful iron gates or carved doors. We saw the home of the head of the Ford

Motor Company in Mexico. And I thought Fords were a low class car!!!

I mentioned before that I never drove in Mexico. Such beeping of horns have I never heard! And confusing!! Intersections were often circles and goodness only knows which way you're supposed to drive. I say, close your eyes and floor it! Aunt Lorraine was so savvy at driving in Mexico. I was amazed at how she got in and out of traffic and knew her way around. She was a great chauffeur. Almost every time she stopped the car, for any reason, there was a little boy cleaning the windshield or selling chiclets, hoping for tips. Also, many adults would roam the streets selling lottery tickets. The lottery was controlled by the Mexican Government.

The next day we went to an Office Supply Store. I have always been nuts about office supplies—addicted I guess. I love new tablets and pens and pencils . . . always buy many things I don't need and always more than I need. At the store in Mexico I bought the kind of bound tablet used in schools there. It is what I put all the notes in from my trip, and as I write this, it is open beside me, bringing back all the memories of the trip. I was astonished at the high prices of office supplies. Most things in Mexico seemed inexpensive compared to the US, but office supplies were not. Across the street from the store was a place where they raised cocks for fighting. We did not attend a cock fight.

Next, we went to a pet shop. I bought a couple of dead bugs to bring back to Mr. Kaddatz, the biology teacher in Clarissa where I was teaching at the time. One was a dead scorpion (alacran), which is poisonous, and the other was a cicada (chicharra), a tropical bug found in Cuernavaca and Acapulco but not in Mexico City because it gets too cold there. Aunt Lorraine said that when they lived in Venezuela the kids used to catch the chicharra and let them crawl on them. They are not poisonous, but I still wouldn't want to have them crawling on me. Scorpions scarred me. Every night I checked all throughout the bed and under the pillow to be sure there were none visiting. Aunt Lorraine said that once she had found a scorpion in a pile of laundry. Wish she hadn't told me that!! The other memorable creature in the pet shop was a huge boa constrictor. I can't even touch a picture of a snake, so I didn't get too close to that cage.

One evening we went to the movie *Gone with the Wind* at a cost of 8 pesos (64 cents at that time). On another evening we saw *Dr. Zhivago* in another (or maybe the same) beautiful theater. At that time it was very common for families to send a chaperone along on dates. We noticed that throughout the theater there were several young couples with a third person along, often appearing to be a mom or older sister. During the trans Siberian train trip in *Dr. Zhivago* it seemed so realistic. Suddenly we realized that the building was moving and for 40 frightening seconds, an earthquake shook us up. Many people got up and left the building, afraid that the high ceiling would collapse I suppose. I remember saying, "My God, Kathy, it's an earthquake!!" We just sat there until it stopped. I don't remember if we saw the rest of the movie or not. It was the first earthquake I had ever felt, and it was a very spooky feeling.

Another interesting shop Aunt Lorraine took us to was Bellas Y Raras, a candle shop. It was where she and Orv had purchased some beautiful candles they brought back for Grandpa and Grandma Felt's 50th wedding anniversary. I have never seen such intricate and unusual candles. We were hoping we could go in the back and see them making the candles, but because of the heat and flammable wax the Mexican Government didn't allow tourists in the factory part of the store. Working conditions must have been pretty bad.

We went with Orv and Lorraine to choir practice one evening. In talking with Lee Sather, an intern at the church, I found that he once sang in a quartet at Luther Seminary in St. Paul with Tom von Fischer, the future husband of my college house mate, Becky Helgeson. Another example of "it's a small world."

The altitude in Mexico City took a bit to get used to. It seemed like I tired easily and was a bit short of breath with not much walking. Funny, I have that now, and the altitude in Shakopee is not much!! Anyway, I noticed this most when we spent the day at the National Museum of Anthropology where we did a lot of walking. It was extremely interesting to see some of Mexico's history. The City was once an island (Tenochtitlan) and still lies on a lake bottom. The building where we would attend the ballet had actually sunk several feet. Zochimilco is the only remnant of floating gardens in Lake of Texcoco. These floating extensions of the islands were built when more room was needed.

The Aztecs actually came to Mexico City because their Gods told them to travel until they found a bird with a snake in its mouth, and there they were to stay. Things would be quite different if they had continued traveling until they got to Minnesota and found a robin with a garter snake in its beak!! The Pyramid (I didn't know Mexico had pyramids until I went there) of the Sun is designed so that on a certain date and time each year it casts NO shadow. The present day Government buildings are erected above (on top of) the former Square of the Aztecs. The Cathedral, for example, is built atop a buried pyramid built for sun worship.

While building the first subway system in Mexico City they found many artifacts and tunnels which dated back to the 1500's. They planned to preserve these and make subway rides like going through a museum. I don't know if that happened or not. I was most amazed at the museum to find that the Aztecs were very advanced in medicine. They removed cataracts and tumors. It was interesting to see their surgical tools and realize that so much was lost when that civilization was lost. I recall being very fascinated with the museum. I don't know that I had ever read or studied much about the Aztecs or Mexico for that matter. As a side note, the brochure you received when entering the museum had specific instructions and diagrams on the back showing how to use the vending machines in the lunchroom area. I had a feeling vending machines were something new at that time.

Finally, we had a sunny day. Aunt Lorraine designated it a day of marketing. We went to the fruit and vegetable market and the meat market. I couldn't believe my eyes. I had never been to an outside market, though they are now quite common in Minnesota in the summer and fall. We bought figs and avocados, papaya, melons, bananas, peppers, cauliflowers, peas and potatoes. Then we bought asparagus, limes and the biggest, juiciest oranges I had ever seen. At the meat market, all of the meat was cut and trimmed as you ordered it. It maybe took longer, but you went home with exactly what you wanted. That is, if your Spanish was good. It was fun to watch Lorraine speaking in Spanish and negotiating the markets and giving her requests to the butcher. Orv, Lorraine and their kids all spoke Spanish fluently as I recall and probably still remember it when needed.

We drove up and out of Mexico City (it is a city in a valley on top of a mountain!) to the Maja Pottery Factory one sunny Friday morning. The drive was unbelievably beautiful. Next to wealth and beauty, would be hundreds of shacks perched on hills, held up by very little. Accommodations? Usually 1-2 rooms and a 'path.' The factory itself was interesting. There were two fellows making the pieces, a couple at the huge ovens overseeing the firing of the pieces, and two more people doing the hand painting. The painting was especially fun to watch. The scenes were of dainty birds, delicate flowers, and breathtaking landscapes. They didn't seem to be typically what I would recognize as Mexican Pottery, more European I thought.

Imagine having the girl scout troop meet at your home? Well, one day Lorraine hosted the troop and it turned out to be memorable. One lady who was to pick up four of the girls and give them rides home was unable to do so as she was in the hospital having her baby—not due that day. She had sent her husband to pick up the girls. On his way, while going through the subway construction zone, there was a cave in and he and his car fell in. Lorraine made at least a dozen calls and found rides home for all of the girls, except the one whose father was in a hole and mother was in the hospital. The girl spent the night with all of us. Her father called later in the evening to say he was out of the sink hole, and they had a baby boy.

Later that same evening the Sather's, from Orv and Lorraine's church, called. They were trying to find the house as they were going to spend the evening but had gone to the wrong address. The wrong address was actually the house where a man had been killed the night before. Anyway they found us, and we spent the evening playing the board game Tripoly and visiting.

Saturday, June 29, was the day designated for Americans in Mexico City to celebrate the 4th of July. There was a parade. Because this was held within the compound/campus at the American School, they went around the field track twice—probably to make it last longer. There was a speech by the Ambassador of the US to Mexico, Fulton Freeman. There was a small fair set up, and hot dogs were 2 pesos each. When they played the National Anthem I was kind of overwhelmed. I had never been outside of the US when it was played. I realized how lucky I was to have been born in such a great country. The best part of the celebration to me was the mariachi band. They are strolling musicians with guitars and violins and trumpets. Their outfits were spectacular with lots of silver buttons and chains and trims, with huge festive sombreros. At the end of the sunny day, we came home sunburned and tired, but we had had a wonderful 4th of July, Mexico style.

Sunday rolled around again. Kathy and I had been to choir practice, so we sang in the choir at Church. Reverend Krause, a Professor at Augsburg Seminary in Mexico City was the guest pastor. Lorraine characterized him as "a bit of a rebel, with his beard and all, but truly a great man." What a 60's kinda statement. He was a wonderful speaker. He came down the aisle to speak close to the people and gave his sermon sitting down on a chair in front of the pulpit. For communion he put on a different robe that was very elaborate. I found out later it was a gift from a Norwegian pastor friend of his. They offered Communion that morning either from a common cup or from individual cups. It was the first time I had seen communion offered from a common cup, except at a Catholic wedding once. That reminds me, the church had kneeling benches too, something I had never before seen in a Lutheran Church.

The next day we went shopping at the Green Door. It was literally a green door on an otherwise nondescript building. There wasn't even a sign saying what was inside. To get in you had to pull a wrinkled up piece of twine attached to an old wire bell, and they would come and let you in. Once inside it was unbelievable. Like my sister Karen said, "It isn't a store, it is an experience." Everything inside was piled to the ceiling or tucked under the shelves on the floor and covered with dust. You literally "pawed" your way through the place. They had carvings, pictures, sombreros, jewelry, copper, pottery, pinatas, dolls, figurines, table clothes, baskets and oodles of junk. What a fun time we had! I bought silver charms, cuff links and other jewelry, carved bookends, a jackass (wood carving) and maracas. The poor salesgirl collected everything as we grabbed it, and we paid for it all in another room when we were done shopping. After shopping at the Green Door we went to a cafe called Shirley's. Just after we had ordered, Orv walked in. I guess businessmen have to eat too. Shirley's was the only place they had found that served pie as we know it. As much as I love pie, I opted for a huge slab of watermelon. Lunch in Mexico was mid-afternoon, and dinner was much later in the evening than we were used to.

My cousin Barb was 10 years old when we were there. She was the oldest of Orv and Lorraine's children. One day we went shopping, and Lorraine let Barb and I go to another part of the area while she ran some errands. We agreed to meet on a particular corner at a certain time. Somehow we got our wires crossed, and Barb and I spent an hour standing on the corner waiting for Lorraine, and she spent that same length of time on another corner waiting for us. I had no clue where we were, so we stayed put and hoped Lorraine would find us. Fortunately, she finally decided to leave the corner and go in search of us. This was waaaaaay before cell phones, so we all spent a lot of time in those days waiting to meet up with others in the US too.

Another day was spent at a market. This time the San Juan Market. If we didn't see it or buy it, it just didn't exist. I've never seen so much stuff. Most of the merchants spoke enough English to make bargaining a lot of fun. San Juan Market was set up by the Government and used mainly by tourists. Afterwards we went to eat at Shakey's Pizza. This was a popular pizza chain in the US at that time. We were all there and I remember paying the bill which was only about $16 US for lots and lots of pizza. We went to Shakey's again a few days later with Beverly and 8 of her little girlfriends to celebrate her birthday which was the 6th of July.

The Pink Zone was a popular section of the city called the Niza District. It is an a "way out" section of the city where the rich, the odd and the snoopy hang out. I wonder which category we fit in? For the Olympics many of the building facades were actually painted pink. Then there was the Bazaar Salado. This seemed to be the rich man's bazaar where movie stars and important dignitaries and rich locals often shopped. We didn't buy much there.

We met Bob and Sheilla, good friends of Orv and Lorraine's, from Canada. We spent an evening at their home with their family, played some ping pong and visited. They had two little girls. Years and years later I would bake the wedding cake for one of their daughters as they had moved to Edina, MN just a few blocks from us. By then Orv and Lorraine had moved to Burnsville, MN. They still keep in touch with Bob and Sheilla, and their families are very close.

On Sunday, June 7, we went to Charreada, a Mexican style rodeo. It was hosted this particular Sunday by the National Association of Charros honoring US Independence Day and the American Community in Mexico. The US Ambassador was the guest of honor. There was the Mexican version of bulldogging, bronco riding and trick roping. The charros (cowboys) were dressed in brilliant costumes. Their horses were also adorned with colorful items. There were young girls performing precision riding and strolling mariachis. There were also local radio and television stars there, and regional dances were performed by students from the Association's School of dance. The funniest thing was the bull flipping competition. The charros would ride their horses next to the bulls, then twist their tails to flip them over.

As much as I enjoyed the Charreada (rodeo), I was more intrigued by the bull fight that we attended. We had box seats that were covered with more box seats above ours. The ceiling was so low I couldn't stand up straight without hitting my head. The stadium was packed. There were three matadors and 6 bulls to be fought. The first fight seemed pretty ordinary. The second bull that pranced into the ring, took a look around, and turned around and went back out the door he had entered from. Moments later he reappeared much to the joy of the shouting and applauding crowd. When he came back in the bull eventually picked up the matador with his horns and injured the matador (gored). He had to be carried from the ring on a stretcher. The 3rd bullfighter had to finish the bull for the injured matador. The next matador took 7 times before he got the sword in right and killed the bull. Another person, called a pickador, goes up to the bulls and puts colorful picks into the upper neck of the bull, I think to weaken the bull. Sometimes the picks stick in the hide of the bull and hang there. The 5th bull was the most fun. At one point the matador was being chased by the bull. He jumped over the 5' fence to get away from the bull. Well, seconds later the bull flipped over the same fence. That's a lot of beef to go over a 5' fence. As serious as it was, it was pretty funny. The crowd went wild. In the bull fight, the bull always loses!! When we were there, 5 of the 6 bulls were killed by one matador, who was given a tour of the ring. This is the first reward. Second is an ear from the bull; third is two ears, and then the tail. The ultimate reward for the very best bullfighter is a hoof!! So do you display those in your den? As horrible as it sounds to watch the killing of the bull, the saving grace is that the meat supposedly was given to the poor.

Another big event was at the 'sinking' Belles Artes to see the Ballet Folklorico de Mexico. This is the building that is built on the lake bed and is sinking. At one time there were steps up to the entrance of the building, but when we were there you actually went down slightly into the building. They had brought experts from around the globe trying to find a solution to the problem of the sinking building with no success at that time.

The costumes, action and music at the Ballet Folklorico were fantastic. My favorite dance was the deer dance, which typified two hunters chasing after the deer. The dance was wild and extremely difficult . . . and fantastic. There was a wedding dance, which was beautiful and accompanied by soft marimba music. The finale was Christmas in Jalisco where they ended up tossing streamers everywhere. Pretty festive. And the final music? What else, but The Mexican Hat Dance!!! What a fantastic show.

After the ballet, we drove through the Zocolo where the Government Square, Palace, and Cathedral are located. It was dark and the best time to see it because on weekends they lit up the entire area. Every part of every building seemed to have lights on them. It was spectacular.

Just when I thought we had seen about everything of interest, Lorraine pulls out her list and says that the next day we would be going to Cuernovoca, then a day later the pyramids, then a day at the Castle and yet another day at the floating gardens at Xochimilco. I doubt that anybody is a better tour guide than Lorraine. She had a plan and showed us about every place of interest in the area.

When we went down the mountain to Cuernovoca, we went from fog and smog to beautiful clear sunshine and fresh air. We went to a fantastic Casino Hotel just to look around. We definitely saw how the other half lived and knew which half we were. There were 4 pools in the hotel and each and every room had a huge patio. Cuernovoca is said to be where many changes in the Catholic Church in Mexico have taken place, They have a Mariachi Mass every Sunday night. Mariachi Mass became very popular back then. Cortez's Palace is also in Cuernovoca. Some of the most exciting driving occurred in Cuernovoca. Lorraine took a quick trip down the wrong way on a one-way street. We gave her such a hard time. On the way home we did our favorite thing in the car—we sang!! That was something we often did while driving to and from our destinations.

Next on Lorraine's itinerary was Chapultepec Castle. The Castle was built by Maximillion of France for his wife—good old "Carly", Carlotta. It was very impressive. We visited the Castle on July 11, which was my sister Kathy's 16th birthday. Flowers were plentiful and inexpensive. She received 9 dozen long stemmed roses, most from her Uncle Orv. We bought her a miniature hand-blown glass baby grand piano which unfortunately did not travel well. When she opened it upon our return to Minnesota, it was in a million pieces.

The last few days in Mexico were filled with more touring. We went to the pyramids. Who knew they had pyramids in Mexico? Not me. That was very interesting. We learned that it was probably a good thing that Orv worked a lot and didn't go with us sightseeing. He went along to the pyramids and couldn't believe that with the majesty of them and history, all us women folks wanted to do was find the nearest shops!! We also visited the farm run by Orv's company.

After almost 4 weeks in Mexico City we began to pack for our return to Minnesota. As sorry as we were to leave, Orv and Lorraine were probably looking forward to getting their life back to normal. We had such a great time we all wished we could stay longer. On July 14 we got back on a plane and left Mexico City. It was an uneventful flight until a stewardess (now they are called flight attendants) with two left feet dumped milk all over my green double knit dress. Yes, we traveled in dresses in the 60's, not like people dress for airplanes trips now. We got off the plane with bags and packages and carry ons that would probably not be allowed today. We looked like typical tourists. Amazing how much stuff you can get into a straw bag or two . . . souvenirs inside souvenirs.

I was in the line at US Customs with a Catholic nun, dressed in full black and white habit, right behind me. When they asked if I had any liquor in my suitcase, I answered loudly that "I don't drink so certainly didn't buy any liquor in Mexico." I think I wanted the nun to know I was a good girl. As I was closing my suitcase, the Customs Agent asked the nun the same question. She quietly said, "I have a few bottles of wine." I felt kinda stupid.

When we landed in San Antonio, Lloyd Dosdall was at the airport to meet us. We spent the afternoon (it was over 102 degrees) at the Hemis-Fair, had a great dinner with him and his wife, spent the night and left for Minnesota early the next morning. The Ford looked pretty good. Suddenly we all became anxious to get home. We crossed Texas, Oklahoma, Kansas and Nebraska in some of the worst heat I have ever experienced. The days were over 100 degrees, and the nights only cooled off a few degrees. The Ford worked fine, but the air conditioning was what we used to call 4-60—drive with all 4 windows open, 60 miles an hour. We would find a motel in the middle of the afternoon when it was the hottest, check in, strip and lie naked on the beds waiting for the air conditioning to cool us off. We filled the bathroom sink with ice and threw in fruit and cans of pop. We got up and left at about 4:00 a.m. to get some driving in before daylight and the baking sun. After spending the night in air conditioned comfort, opening the door to go out in the morning was like walking into a furnace. We just plugged on down the road, windows wide open, silently cussing everyone who passed us with their windows shut—obviously enjoying air conditioning. Now most cars come with air conditioning as standard equipment. In the 60's it was an option that I didn't have in my Ford. I never bought another car without air conditioning!

The month in Mexico City was a wonderful experience. We got to be part of Orv and Lorraine's family for awhile. They were wonderful hosts. We were excited when they moved back to Minnesota, so we could see them more often. In fact, we helped them a little when they moved back to Minnesota in 1971 and their household shipment arrived from Mexico. Karen and I went with Lorraine to buy the first groceries for the house. I remember several shopping carts full of groceries and being shocked that it was over $200. In the 70's $200 was a lot of cash and bought a station wagon full of groceries!! We were talking and laughing when we left the grocery store and drove off without driving through the lane to have them put the groceries in our car. We had to turn around and go back to pick them up.

Chapter 3

There's Someone for Everyone

(What Led Me to Korea and My Husband of 35 Years)

"With my luck, if there really is someone for everyone, my someone is probably on the other side of the world, and I'll never find him," I shared with my early teenage friends as we sat in the convertible my dad had pulled into our gravel driveway in front of the house. He sold Chevrolets in our town of 350 people, and we were too young to drive, but I recall the day we sat in the convertible with the top down and discussed boys.

In the 50's, the *facts of life* consisted of mom saying that "When you get your first *monthly visitor*, the supplies are in the closet next to the vanity in our bedroom." So, besides talking about our future husbands that day in the hot July sun, we also talked about how girls became pregnant. We ruled out kissing because we had seen some of the cheerleaders and basketball players kissing after the games, and none of the girls got pregnant (so we thought at the time). We recalled that a couple of girls in our school were out of school for a few weeks, and when they returned they had had "appendectomies" but *no babies.* We finally decided, unanimously, that babies were caused by kissing, but only married women became pregnant when participating in the act because God knows who is married and who is not. We had solved one of the great mysteries of growing up and were glad we had done so. We piled out of the convertible and went back to the neighbor's porch to resume playing with our paper dolls.

A few years later I learned to drive on a Sunday afternoon in a 1938 Plymouth with my friend Carol riding shotgun. She had never driven a straight stick car (manual transmission to you youngsters), but she knew how to drive a tractor that you had to shift, so she figured she could teach me what she knew. Her parents were spending the afternoon at my parent's home. They all sat in the front room of the house looking out the picture window and enjoying us driving back and forth. Every time we turned around a couple of blocks down the street, we had to go up a small incline. This was problematic for me. Each time, we would turn the car off, put on the emergency brake and Carol would get in the driver's seat to get us up the hill and back on the street. We jerked and lurched at each corner, and I killed the engine numerous times. But, by the end of the afternoon we could drive smoothly past the picture window without our heads lashing back and forth and impressed our parents with our progress. To this day it is still a challenge for me to drive a straight stick, but I can do it unless there are hills involved. My dad sold the '38 Plymouth a few weeks later. The buyer had it about a week and the transmission went out. Wonder what happened???

I took, and passed my driver's test in an automatic '55 Chevy. The accelerator pedal was missing, but if you held your foot just right, you could use the metal that once held the pedal, and it worked fine. One of my friends drove over the flags on her first driver's test, signaled right but turned left, and had troubles driving, but eventually passed and is still on the roads out in West Central Minnesota, so beware. Carol passed her test too, but not on a tractor!

After high school graduation I went 150 miles away to a small church college in Minneapolis called Augsburg. It was Norwegian Lutheran with a token Swede here or there. I went to chapel almost every day and took Norwegian as my foreign language. I don't think Augsburg is conservative now, but it sure was then. The first college dance at Augsburg was when I was a junior or senior. The dance was to be at the spring formal, called the JS (Junior-Senior), but it had never been followed by the word "dance". It was held at a downtown hotel ballroom. The room was lined with alumni who were there to witness the historic event.

I graduated with a degree in Business Education and went to a small rural town in north central Minnesota, Clarissa, to teach for 6 years before growing tired of the small town. It was a wonderful 6 years but seemed like it was time to move on. Sitting in the teacher's lounge with other faculty members after school one day I was mentioning that it was time to move on to something else, somewhere else. A co-worker said "Why don't you apply to teach overseas with the Department of Defense (DOD) and see the world? That is what I plan to do after I get my 2 years of required stateside teaching completed."

After a grueling interview process I was offered a teaching job in Korea for the DoD (Department of Defense) schools for dependents of U.S. Military Personnel stationed overseas. I received the job offer from the Department of Defense via a registered letter from the Pentagon. In the little town of Clarissa, this caused quite a stir. The postmaster actually delivered the letter to my classroom at the school during the day. He had me sign for the letter and then sort of stood there, no doubt waiting to find out what this important letter could possibly be. Poor guy. I thanked him and did not open the document until he was back at the post office. In fact, I did not share the news with anyone in Clarissa until after Easter break which was a few weeks later. I requested the next day off as personal leave and drove to Willmar for the day to discuss the job offer with my mom and dad. After locating Korea on the map and realizing it was actually connected to North Korea and China, I accepted the offer. I generally knew where Korea was but had to be sure. I just couldn't imagine turning down the offer, no matter how remote the location, and always wondering what life would have been like if I had accepted. I had no idea what a life-changing decision that would be.

The interview process was nothing compared to the 39-hour trip from my parent's home in Willmar, Minnesota, to Busan, Korea. We left Willmar in mom and dad's car and arrived at the airport in Minneapolis two hours later. After a flight to San Francisco, I boarded a Greyhound bus for Travis Air Force Base to await the MAC (Military Airlift Contract) Flight to Korea. The flight included a stop in Anchorage for fuel, a stop at Yokota AFB (Air Force Base) in Japan to drop off some military personnel, and finally touching down in Osan AFB in Korea, *The Land of the Morning Calm,* as was printed on a sign above the doorway into the terminal. After processing into the country, we boarded a bus for Seoul. The bus was EXACTLY like the ones I had seen on the MASH TV series for years . . . they really had kept these buses running for years and years? After getting my luggage onto the bus and settling into my seat for what would now be a dusty and bumpy couple of hours, we were told that there was an alert, and we wouldn't be leaving the base until they were sure it was safe to do so. Excuse me, but wasn't the war over? My God, I thought, what have I gotten myself into? We were told to get down, so we couldn't be seen through the bus windows, preferably to get down on the floor under the seats. In a dress, with nylons (no panty hose—ya, you guessed it—garters!!!) I decided to lay down on the seat and take my chances. I don't think my bulk would have fit under the seat anyway. The alert was because some North Korean gorillas were believed to have infiltrated the northern border (the DMZ—Demilitarized Zone dividing North and South Korea) and were lurking somewhere nearby. After a few minutes they sounded the all-clear (like the end of a tornado warning in Minnesota telling us to come back out of our basements), and we left the base for the drive to Seoul. At that point I wasn't at all sure I ever wanted to leave the base, but I had no choice.

We arrived in Seoul at Youngsan Compound in a driving rainstorm and got a base taxi to take me to the train station for my 8 hour trip to Busan where I would be living. Then I boarded the "blue" train which was the nicer train used by tourists and more affluent locals instead of the "red" train which was the cheap rides for locals. Somehow I envisioned chickens in crates and lots of other animals and produce on board the "red" train. I never did ride the "red" train. The "blue" train was very nice. Seats were plush, large windows gave fantastic views of the Korean countryside, and I enjoyed the ride. We stopped in only a couple of cities during the 8-hour trip. Vendors would come on board and sell everything from peanuts, to apples, to tangerines (the best I've ever eaten in my life!) and beverages. And, of course, I am still in the same suit of clothes I had on when I left Willmar with my parents the day before. The garters are now embedded in my chubby thighs and not comfortable.

I was met in Busan by the High School Principal, Chet, who had a military van and took me to the base. The driving rain was even worse in Busan, and the trees were leaning over in the wind. We were in the midst of a serious tropical storm. Again I thought, what have I gotten myself into? Thank goodness we didn't have cell phones in the 70's. I would have called somebody by hen and called off the whole darn trip.

Chronology of the Trip—Willmar, MN to Busan, Korea

(39 hours in the same peach double knit dress, nylons w/garters but sensible shoes, thank God!)

Willmar to Mpls	private car	3 hours	cried all the way and so did Mom and Dad
Mpls to S.F.	airplane	4 hours	cried all the way
S.F. to Travis AFB, CA	bus	3 hours	fewer tears, more excitement
Travis AFB to Osan AFB in Korea with a	airplane	17 hours	no tears, plane full of mostly men, not bad!

fueling stop in Alaska and short layover in Japan—Yokota AFB

Osan to Youngsan	bus	2 hours	f e a r a n d apprehension

Youngsan to Seoul Public Train Station	taxi	1 hours	first ride in public transportation, interesting
Seoul to Busan	"blue" train	8 hours	adventurous, fun exciting
Busan Train Station to Hialeah Army Base	Army van	1 hour	relief

I was finally at what would be my home for the next 2 years. (I still have the peach colored double knit dress I wore on the 39-hour trip.) Hialeah Compound was a very small Army base in Busan on the southeast coast of Korea. Once in Busan I was the head of the Business Department. That sounds impressive, but the school was so small that I WAS the Business Department. Each discipline had it's own quansit hut with covered sidewalks leading from one to another and to the "front office" where the Principal reigned, with a secretary who was usually the wife of an officer living on the base.

I had one hut just for all of my classes. I had a general business class—a lot of practical stuff—and basic math. I recall that when we came to a chapter on reading utility meters and paying bills, some of the students had never seen a meter and had no clue that people actually had to pay for water or electricity every month. They had lived in military housing their entire lives, and the utilities were always provided, along with the housing.

I enjoyed the free housing and utilities those two years I spent in Korea—making almost all of my income disposable. Medical needs and dental needs were provided on base. I sold my car when I went to Korea and bought a bicycle when I got there, so I had no car payment or car insurance or gas to buy. My only expenses were $5 a week for a housemaid who came every day to clean, wash laundry by hand in the kitchen sink, and do a little cooking; $10 a month to have a "sew" girl come in for a week; and food and personal items. And, of course, lots of shopping and eating out.

The "sew" girl was the greatest pleasure for a too tall and too big person like me. All I had to do was give her a picture of what I wanted her to sew. She made my wedding dress for which she charged me $15 extra. I would provide the material and she would take my measurements, with a lot of exclamations in Korea that probably were "wow" regarding the amount of the measuring tape it took to get around me to measure. Then she would cut out the fabric, no patterns, and I would go home for lunch and she would try the garment on me. When I got home from school in the afternoon the outfit would be ready, unless it was extra complicated. Each month I could pretty much count on 5 new outfits. And, they all fit, they were big enough and long enough, and I got any style I wanted. Talk about Heaven right here on earth. For a tall, robust Norwegian this was Paradise!!

I taught typing to a class of 10 students. The typewriters were secured in locked mesh cabinets in the back of the classroom, and each day the students had to get out their huge manual typewriters and lug them to their desks for class. We had extra typewriters which was good because the janitor, Mr. Kim, was also our typewriter repairman. He stole parts from other machines to keep at least 10 working at all times. We were at a military base considered a "hardship tour" due to the fact that you could not get out of the country without first getting to Seoul which was 200+ miles away. Nowadays you can fly right out of Busan, but you couldn't at that time because it was not an International Airport. Well, we were at the end of the supply line too, and typewriter ribbons were a scarce commodity. We used and reused them until you almost couldn't read the typing.

I also taught a class in Economics and in Business Law—6 students in that class. I learned a lesson quickly regarding how wonderful the Korean people are about recycling and reusing items. Nothing was easily thrown away. I prepared a test for the Economics class and had extra copies which I just threw away. A couple of weeks later I went to a vegetable market near the Base and bought apples. When I got home and tore open the bag of apples, which was a white paper bag, lo and behold the inside of the bag was my Economics test.

There were other ways that the Koreans were "green" way before it ever occurred to us here in the U.S. The Koreans used to bid on purchasing the trash from the base. The high bid won the contract and paid the U.S. Military for their trash. When the truck went through the Base collecting the garbage, the back of the truck was filled with boxes and bins and 50 or 100 gallon drums and several workers who sorted and organized the trash as they rolled down the street. Hence, I found out how my extra Economic tests became bags for produce at the local market.

I also taught Accounting and Shorthand. All of my classes had 10 students or less. In some ways that was more difficult to motivate myself as a teacher than if there were 35 students. Did I just say bigger is better? Yup. I always taught better in a full room rather than having a small number of students.

I supervised the yearbook staff and school paper staff and chaperoned a dance or two. I had students in the business work program, and they had jobs at the radio station, computer lab, theater and other places on the Base. The student working in the computer building had an interesting workplace—the military told us that the building was wired to be blown up in case of infiltration, so the computers would not be compromised. I didn't ever stay in that building any longer than I had to.

While living there we were told to have a suitcase packed, including a small amount of cash, and be ready for immediate evacuation should the North Koreans decide to "come on down." We actually had an evacuation drill, just like a fire drill. This was a whole lot spookier in my opinion.

I was in Korea when the U.S. Military went from script (play money we called it, but in the same denominations as greenbacks) to "green"—regular U.S. currency. Script was actually *Military Payment Certificates*, commonly known as MPC, a substitute for American money paid to American *military* personnel serving in foreign countries. It seemed to be used in order to keep tabs on the black market which was alive and well in any country with U.S. Military presence. Of course the

GI's had access to lots of U.S. products that were not easily found in many countries as they are now. It seemed that when the Military bosses felt there was too much money being used in the black market, they would change to different script.

One morning when I awoke to my clock radio, tuned in to the Military radio station, I sat up with a start. The voice said, "Attention all U.S. Personnel in the Republic of Korea, Attention all . . . ." and repeated it several times. Then they said we were all supposed to report to our duty stations immediately. We were to bring all of our script with us. They announced that the base was closed for 24 hours, nobody in or out, all base operations were closed, including the PX (post exchange—kinda like Target), theater, laundry, officers club, etc., etc. School was closed too. When we got to our duty station, there were accountants there with greenbacks to be exchanged for our script. We had to write our name, rank and serial number (Social Security Number in civilians cases) on EACH bill and turn them in for regular U.S. greenbacks. Of course, I had just cashed my paycheck the day before and had a huge stack of bills. Because everything was closed, we had the rest of the day to spend with friends on post playing board games, watching TV and just having impromptu pot lucks. It was like a snow day with no snow.

Anybody dealing in the black market, outside the base, who had a lot of script was out of luck because they had no way to get on post with the script in order to change it for green. There were even rumors of bags of script being thrown over the fences surrounding the base in hopes of getting some of their money back. To my knowledge, Korea was the last country to have script and has had green ever since. Once imports of U.S. Products became more and more prevalent, the black market became less and less attractive. That is probably why the U.S. switched to green.

Liquor was probably the most sought after U.S. product desired by Koreans and so GI's would buy their maximum amount of bottles, as shown on their ration card, and sell it for many times their cost, thus turning a nice profit. My roommate and I were very popular because everybody knew we didn't drink and our ration cards went unused. They were like gold. Once in awhile we would let one of the other teachers use our ration card but were careful not to support the black market.

One time my mom wrote a letter and asked me if it was safe for me to walk alone at night "over there." I told her it was safer than anyplace in the U.S. There were no gangs that I knew of, murders and rapes were almost non-existent and with nobody carrying guns, except the military and police, it was very safe. However, a 1-foot deep hole in the back yard of a neighbor's house actually made walking in the dark at night dangerous, especially the night I stepped in it and probably caused the first earthquake ever felt in that city. Another dangerous thing about walking alone at night was low hanging clotheslines, but that's another story.

Each spring when people packed who were leaving Korea, those of us who knew we were staying for the next school year would buy window air conditioner units, bikes, and anything else people felt like leaving behind. We would buy it, put it in our assigned housing for the next school year, along with our other personal items, then head home for the summer, at Government expense.

The beauty shop on the base was a wonderful experience. Not only did you get a shampoo/set, permanent wave, or cut, but while you were under the dryer they would give you a full neck and upper back massage. Pedicures included leg and foot massages, plus shaving your legs. However, the first time I had my legs shaved at the beauty shop, I think my eyes got as big as saucers when the gal came at me with a straight edge razor and gave me the smoothest legs of my life. Their curling irons were metal rods heated on a hot plate type of unit. I had a hair dryer that I brought along but seldom used. However, when it did quit working, I just threw it in the garbage because it was a very cheap one, and I was sure it wasn't worth fixing. However, the next day I found it on the cupboard. The housemaid had taken it out of the garbage. She said, "I can have man fix for you." So I said, "Sure", and she brought it back a few days later. It worked fine and cost me $2.

We did a lot of sightseeing around Korea and in Japan during the two school years I was over there. The people were so friendly and helpful in Korea that it was never a hassle to go out and about. Japan was different. We felt like they would just as soon never even deal with us. I also felt even bigger in Japan than I did in Korea. The Korean race is larger than the Japanese and other SE Asian races. In Korea there were lots of men 6' tall and lots of larger people, which surprised me. In fact, when I told my parents I was going to marry a Korean man my mom's 1st question was, "How tall is he?" I think she had visions of a real Mutt and Jeff couple. However, I'm 6'1" and my husband 5'10" or 11" so not much of a difference. In Japan, however, I think I could stand in the middle of a crowd with my arms stretched straight out, do a 360 and not hit anybody—they would all be below my armpits! I won't even begin to tell you how much I enjoyed folding up this bulk of protoplasm into taxis in Korea and Japan.

In 2003 Joon went to the wedding in Korea of his friend's son. He met his friend through Northwest—his friend working for NW in Osaka. He was asked to give a toast at the reception. He asked me for ideas on what he could say, via e-mail from Korea, and this is what I sent him:

Date: 12/9/2003 9:46 AM
Sender: Phyllis D. Chi
To: JKChi@aol.com
Subject: Ideas for wedding speech

Joon,

Some ideas (this was easy once I thought about it—the things that made me love you)

Say to the Groom:
I've been married for 29 years . . . all of them to the same woman! I asked my wife for ideas for what to say for this wedding and she said "It is simple . . . for a successful marriage, just find the right woman!!! I think you have done that.

Say to both of them:
Really, the secret to a long and happy marriage is simple to say, but you must both work on it always to make it happen.

• You must always **love** each other and show it in your actions and how you treat each other. Don't be afraid to say it now and then, but "actions are better than words" so live it daily!

• You must always **trust** each other because it is the basis of an ongoing strong relationship. Let each other have their own space . . . have things you do together, but other things that you do with others . . . variety is the spice of life.

• You must always **support** each other because anything that is good for your spouse is probably good for you. The bad times are easier if you support each other and the good times are even better!!!

• You must be **honest** with each other and share your feelings and concerns and joys and sorrows. Sometimes we find difficulty in communicating because we are afraid if we say exactly what we mean that somehow our spouse won't understand. However, it is usually better to be open and honest about your feelings from the beginning so hurt feelings don't have a chance to grow into hatred.

• And last, **laugh** at yourselves, laugh at the funny things in life and laugh often . . . it is a wonderful way to release tension and get through some of the more difficult times. Don't be afraid to be angry, just don't STAY angry. See the humor in your shortcomings.

Say this as a toast at the end of your speech:

"Let's toast the bride and groom and wish them good luck for a long and happy life . . . it is like a flight with a little turbulence. It is ok as long as the landing is safe."

This pretty much sums up how I really feel about marriage. We are now in year 35 of our marriage and going strong. We must be doing something right!

Chapter 4

I Do, I Do, I Finally Do

(Three Weddings to the Same Man)

Not many women marry the same man 3 times, get to wear their wedding dress a couple of times and get married on two sides of the world. I did, to Joon Kwi Chi. We set our wedding date for August 4, 1974. We had 3 weddings. NONE of them were on August 4, 1974. We were legally married at the US Embassy in Seoul, Korea on May 31, 1974. Our August 4, 1974 wedding to be held in Willmar, Minnesota was postponed a week before that date because Joon had not received his passport. Our second wedding was in Seoul in October, and our last wedding was in Willmar, Minnesota in December. At least all of our weddings were in the same year.

I was spending the summer with my parents in Willmar, planning the wedding, attending showers, and generally having a lot of fun. That all came to a screeching halt on a Tuesday morning the week before the wedding. Joon called early in the morning to say that he did not have his passport and would not be getting it any time soon. His background check was delayed due to checking on a brother who was taken to North Korea during the Civil War and was still missing. I hung up the phone in disbelief and went into mom and dad's bedroom to share the news. We were all stunned. Mom said I should call him back and tell him he couldn't postpone it. She was not taking it well!! And, mom and I were going to the Sevig's cabin on Lake Spicer in the afternoon for a shower mom's friends were holding in my honor.

By noon we had been to the church to reschedule the wedding for Christmastime, called and postponed the flowers and the cake to the new date and picked up cards to send to the 200+ guests to uninvite them. There were some who wondered if this meant we would be calling it all off. Little did they know that we had already been legally married as of the previous May 31, 1974. Over the summer I had done all of the notifications to Social Security, my bank, etc. to change everything to my married name, even my MN driver's license had been changed. Only our families and our pastor knew that we were already legally married.

When I began packing to return to Korea for my second school year in Busan, mom was sitting on the edge of the bed talking. I had purchased a new negligee for my wedding night. Mom and I discussed whether or not I should take it with me. We agreed that Joon and I would have to discuss our living arrangements, but in my mind we weren't really married until the church wedding which was now scheduled for December of 1974. We had already planned a fall ceremony in Seoul, Korea, so I also packed my wedding dress. Because I had my dress made in Korea and mom wasn't along, I waited until I got back to Willmar, and she and I went shopping and bought the bridal veil and put it together. It was so pretty. And, when our son got married 30 years later his bride used parts of it for her veil. Besides the veil, mom and I bought shoes for me. I ended up buying white slippers—didn't need any more height and wanted lots of comfort. Plus, nobody would see them anyway.

We found out much later that one person had showed up for our August wedding and that was Aunt Annie, my grandfather Felt's brother's wife. She was quite elderly and had her daughter or granddaughter bring her from the Itasca Park area of Minnesota to Willmar. They spoke with the pastor at the church then turned around and went back home. Aunt Annie was a wonderful lady. She had made a small tablecloth for us and cross stitched a design. I still have that gift and treasure it.

We left all of the arrangements for an August wedding intact . . . . so a summer wedding was held in December. The pale pink bridesmaid's dresses were beautiful against the deep red poinsettias and evergreens that flanked the altar. The wedding pictures were even better with the same background. My dad took the napkins back to the stationary store and told them to "run them through again" so both dates were on the napkins. He wasn't just saving money, but helping keep the history.

Our wedding ended up requiring original invitations, then the un-invites, then the re-invites and then the thank-you cards. The US Postal Service had a good year in 1974.

The weekend the wedding was planned for was not a loss. My dad rented an RV and our family (one sister a couple of years older than me and one a few years younger—neither married at the time) took what would be our last Tinseth family vacation. We drove to South Dakota and the Black Hills. We went to the Passion Play, stopped at Wall Drug on the way, and were all still talking to one another at the end of the trip. At the precise time the wedding was supposed to happen we were sitting at a rodeo in South Dakota, and I was wearing my brand new cowboy hat. I still have that hat and enjoy telling the story behind it.

I flew back to Korea in late August. Remember I was already married—had been since May 31, but was in the middle of a long wait between the marriage and the honeymoon. When I arrived in Seoul Joon was unable to meet my plane, so I took a taxi to the Naija Hotel where he had made a reservation for me. My concerns about our living arrangements were answered when I checked in and went to my room which was a single room with a single bed. No discussion needed on that subject.

We had a wonderful Korean wedding in October and flew back to the US for Christmas Vacation and got married again. We flew into Minneapolis and my parents picked us up. We got to Willmar at 10:00 p.m. on Friday night, Dec. 20, 1974. The next morning we had wedding rehearsal at 9:00 a.m., brunch (groom's dinner?) at a local restaurant after the rehearsal, then back to church to change and took the pictures at noon.

The wedding was at 2:00 p.m. with the reception in the church basement. Our family tradition did not include dances, so after the reception all of the out-of-town guests and closest family and friends went to my parent's home for supper and "fellowship."

At the reception in the church basement, Mom's "circle", the group of ladies from church she met with monthly for Bible Study, provided some of the food and served it as well. Friends from college "opened gifts" and displayed them for everyone to view during the reception. We had cousins serve punch from a sterling silver punch bowl borrowed from mom's friend Lennea. She was so worried about her punch bowl that she hovered in that area the entire afternoon. There were also friends designated to open the gifts and display them so people could look at them during the reception. This was a very traditional type church reception. When we got our wedding pictures, the photographer had taken a picture of the gift table and only then did we realize that it had been strategically placed in front of a Sunday School bulletin board that read "Praise the Lord." Mom and dad gave us money for our wedding gift so that we could buy a set of china in Korea or Japan, which we did. We still have the set and use it on all special occasions. We also bought our 8-panel silk screen with wedding money. Sonja is now the proud owner of that screen. One other great gift we got from mom and dad was a huge white family Bible. Because we had been legally married at the Embassy in Seoul, there was no marriage license for the pastor, witnesses and us to sign, so we all signed in the Bible.

We gave aprons to the servers and corsages to everyone who helped. A friend cut the cake and unlike nowadays there was no charge to cut or serve the cake. Life was pretty simple then, and a wedding did not break the bank. I'm sure mom and dad gave the soloist and organist and preacher a thank you note with money in it but probably only $20 each. There was no charge for using the church we belonged to, and the fancy cake and flowers were in the $200 range. My bouquet consisted of glamelias, a made-up flower consisting of deep red roses positioned in the middle of white gladiola blossoms . . . it made a stunning bouquet.

My cousin Ted was going to sing at our wedding in August, but when we moved the ceremony to December he was unable to schedule it. My dad asked his friend, Bishop Hansen, the Bishop for our church within the Willmar area, to sing. I had specifically asked him to sing Song of Ruth . . . . "my people will be your people and my God, your God" . . . . that one. On his own he decided that he would sing a different song. I was not happy. Anyway, he sang beautifully. Dee played the organ. She was fantastic. We have our ceremony on reel-to-reel but no longer have a machine to play it on. We also have our Korean ceremony on film but no projector to play it on. Such is the downside of new technology.

After the reception, mom and dad invited their closest family and friends over to their house for supper (still not called dinner even though it was in the evening). We joined everyone at their house and then left in dad's car for a few days honeymoon. We drove as far as Minneapolis that evening and were both so tired we found a motel and checked in. There were two double beds in the room, and we each slept in one. We were both pooped. Why pay for two beds and only use one? We are sooooo practical.

I had to do all of the driving to and from Chicago because Joon had no license and had never driven a car. In Korea, public transportation was so great that if you lived in the big city like Joon did a car was not necessary. So I did the driving. We found Joon's friends, the Suk's, and stayed with them overnight. Their guest bedroom was Korean style with no "normal" bed but rather pillows and puffy blankets to make into a bed. Joon let me have all of the pillows but I still was so uncomfortable I didn't sleep well. He spent most of the night visiting with Mr. Suk as they hadn't seen each other for a long time. The next day we went down to the Indiana/Kentucky border to stay with Joon's friend Ron and his Korean wife. Ron is the friend of Joon's who encouraged him to ask me to marry him. It was fun to see them. Then we drove back to Willmar to spend Christmas with my family before returning to Korea.

The ceremony in Korea was a Civil Ceremony held at the Tower Hotel in Seoul. I stayed at the Naija Hotel the night before the wedding and made a huge mistake the morning of the wedding—I went to a hairdresser in the hotel that I had never gone to before. Well, I was in tears by the time she was done styling and went back to the hotel and fixed it the best I could. She just didn't get my hair anywhere near how I wanted it. My roommate Lynda was my bridesmaid. She and I suffered through the morning and got to the Tower Hotel in time for the ceremony. There must have been over 300 guests. At least it looked like it to me. There was a small chamber orchestra playing lovely music, and the main difference in the ceremony, besides the language, was that as each of us came up the aisle an announcer told the audience about us and there was applause now and then.

After the ceremony we marched down the aisle and a beautiful wedding cake had been wheeled in at the end of the aisle. We cut the cake in half with a huge sword. We then went to a room for a special family ceremony where we bowed to my husband's family. His mom threw dried nuts and fruit into my train as I held it in front of me. She also pulled apart a chicken, drank some whiskey and other things that I was not familiar with. But it was a wonderful experience, and she seemed to genuinely enjoy welcoming me into the Chi family. Joon had come over to my hotel the night before and we practiced bowing so I would know what to do the next day for this ceremony with his family. He kinda modified the bowing, so I could even do it.

It was a wonderful day even though I didn't understand much of what was going on. I avoided smiling too widely because in Korean tradition if you do so on your wedding day there is a very good chance that your first born will *not* be a son and that is not great!! I was so nervous I don't think there was any problem keeping very serious. I don't know who selected my bouquet, but it was very pretty, and I still have it dried in a bag in my closet.

I wore my white gown for this ceremony and did not change to my Korean dress. However, for the church wedding in Willmar, I put on my Korean dress during the reception, including a high traditional crown, so I could share that experience with mom and dad's friends and our family.

During the reception a large group of Joon's buddies rounded their chairs and began to do what I called "grill the bride." They wanted to be sure I would take care of him properly. Although the questions shot to me quickly from the circle of friends, I must have had the right answers because they all seemed pleased and finally let me free from the "inquisition." They seemed to enjoy this a whole lot more than I did.

A large group of teachers and friends from the military base that I lived on and taught with in Busan (south eastern coast) took the train along with me for the 8 hour trip to Seoul the Friday before the wedding. On Sunday, the day after the wedding, we all took the train back to Busan. We didn't live together until the church wedding . . . another story for another book at another time.

Chapter 5

Beautiful, Beautiful Brown Eyes

(Special Thoughts About our 3 Children)

Because brown is a dominant trait and my husband is Korean, all of our children were born with beautiful brown eyes.

The children we bear forever change our lives. Our first son, JonNamsun Tinseth Chi, was born March 8, 1976 at Fairview Southdale Hospital in Edina, Minnesota. The labor was long and hard. A heart monitor was inserted under his scalp before he was born to monitor him. They had difficulty inserting the monitor and said it was probably because he had a lot of hair, which he did! A few hours after he was born, the doctor came in to say that he had some heart problems and needed to be transferred to Children's Health Center where he could be cared for by a pediatric cardiologist and a facility designed to care for baby's born with problems like Jon's. We were able to go into the nursery and touch Jon and hold his little hands through "sleeves" built into the incubator he was housed in. He was taken by ambulance to Children's and we would see him there. They moved me to a room in the maternity ward with a mother who had lost her baby. I was released the next day and went straight to Children's with Joon to see Jon. This was the beginning of a 6½-year partnership with Children's, the cardiologist team of Katkov and Singh, a staff of fantastic people, and a God and family and friends who watched over him for those years. He was never expected to survive to his first birthday. We had him for over 6 years.

Erick came next in 1979. Joon had finished his studies at Normandale College in Bloomington and was job hunting. He called home one day to say that he got a job with North Central Airlines, but there was good news and bad news. The good news was that he got the job, as a customer service agent. The bad news was that he would be based out of Chicago for the first year. This was in June of 1979. Jon was 3 and Erick was due in September. This was the summer that Joon's two brothers, their wives and 3 teenagers immigrated from Korea and lived with us. We also had a live-in nanny to help with the kids. Her name was Pam. She was from Hinckley and had been a student of my sister who taught at the high school. Talk about a houseful.

The only person who didn't live there full time was Joon. After training for his new job, he got in his blue Ford one Sunday morning and headed off for Chicago to find a place to live and begin his new job. He barely made it into Wisconsin when his car suffered a serious problem. He turned back, flew to Chicago and took his car later. When he got to Chicago I asked if he had found a place to live. He said, "You know that TV show called *Three's Company*? Well, that is how I'll be living." He had found a furnished apartment shared by other airline employees who lived elsewhere but were based out of Chicago . . . mostly flight attendants and women.

Joon was off work on Tuesdays and Wednesdays. He joked with me and said I had to have the baby on a Tuesday, which I did. On a Monday night in September I went into labor. My mom was staying with us at the time to help out, so I called the doctor first, then Joon and said we were on our way to the hospital. We lived in Bloomington at the time. Joon was at work at O'Hare Airport when I called. He turned to his supervisor and said that his wife was on the way to the hospital. There was a flight leaving for Minneapolis in a little while and Joon was on it. By the time mom and I got to the hospital and checked in, it was only a half hour later that Joon walked into the labor room and joined us.

Erick's labor was uneventful but went on far too long. At 6:00 a.m., Tuesday morning, he finally arrived. To our relief he seemed healthy and robust, but until we made it through the first night, I worried that the doctor would walk in and tell us there was something wrong. Thankfully that did not happen. He was fine!! When it was time to bring him home from the hospital, Joon brought Jon to see Erick and to help get him dressed for the ride home. It was so cute. It began a bond between the two brothers that was very strong.

As Erick got older Jon started calling him "the preacher" because he talked so much. On the night Jon died I asked him if he wanted to see the preacher. He replied "No, I want to see Erick." I think he knew he was leaving us.

I made a big mistake with Erick when Jon died. We decided to take Erick to the funeral home to say goodbye but not to bring him to the funeral. I said that Jon was so sick that he couldn't wake up and would not be able to come home with us any more. Wow, was that a huge mistake!! When Erick was in high school once in awhile he and I would get into deep discussions about lots of things. One night he was late getting home and I was sitting in the kitchen window watching for him. This night we had one of our discussions. One thing that came out of our conversation was that Erick was always afraid to go to sleep and kept his TV and light on in his bedroom all those years. You can guess why . . . going to sleep and not waking up probably terrified him. How I have felt about that is sad, but I am glad we talked about it the way we did.

Erick and I used to have great talks in the car when I took him to confirmation classes. When they were studying the 10 Commandments, we would try and name a law or rule and see if it tied into the 10 Commandments. We never did find one that didn't apply.

When we moved to our house on Aspasia Lane, Erick wanted a basketball hoop in the driveway. My dad, Gramps, helped Erick dig a hole for the pole and mix 900 lbs. of cement. That is not a typo!! Really, that is what the directions said and that is what we did! Erick and Sonja put their initials in the wet cement and that pole will probably outlast the house.

Erick was so darn bright that he didn't ever have to study much to get along. And, he was ok with just getting along. He enjoyed people too much to spend much time with his nose in a book. Little did we know that he actually suffered from Attention Deficit Disorder (ADD) all through school. Unlike most kids with ADD, he still did well. His disruption in class usually was to the delight of the other kids and often the teachers. He was more fun than a problem. His quick wit and photographic mind kept him from being a troublemaker and a failure as a student, the fate of many kids with ADD. In fact, he was in the gifted program in Elementary School. Anyway, when Erick was in college he talked with a Fraternity brother and that friend said maybe Erick had ADD. Erick told us about the discussion, and we made an appointment for him to see our family doctor. Sure enough, he did have ADD and was put on a medication that was very helpful to Erick. In fact, that summer he came home one weekend and was sunburned. I asked what happened. He replied, "For the first time since probably the 3rd grade, I read a book. I was outside in the sun reading and stayed too long." Anyone with ADD knows that concentration is a real problem and sitting down and reading for any length of time is a challenge. We felt bad when we realized he had gone so long without being diagnosed. But looking back on it, I'm not so sure being on drugs for ADD all through school would have been great either. Guess we'll never know.

In 5th grade Erick never took a spelling test. He always got all of the words correct on the pre-test, so the teacher waived the regular test. So, he wasn't always challenged either. He enjoyed not having to work too hard. Just like me when I was in school. I hated having schoolwork interfere with my social life. I was into extra curriculars and all the fun stuff. Classes were secondary. In high school Erick was on student council and often did the morning announcements over the intercom system. He played sports, he was in band—and pretty much drove the band director nuts. He sang in the choir. He was a lot of fun on campus and very well liked. He was often late in getting to school and parked in interesting spots so he could run in before the last bell.

Some of Erick's high school friends also went to the U of M, some also belonged to the same fraternity and many are still close friends with Erick to this day. We are very fortunate that he ran with a good crowd and stayed out of real trouble.

In elementary school Erick and I were in the car one day when I asked him what the phone number was on the back of a truck right in front of us. The number was lots of 8's and 3's, and he couldn't tell the difference. I had been watching him and thought that his eyesight might be lacking. So, the next day I called the school nurse and asked if she would give Erick a vision test and let me know what she thought. She called me later in the afternoon and said, "I just checked Erick's vision, and I'm not sure how he found his way to my office!" So, after school I took him over to Southdale Shopping Center to a 1-hour glasses place and got him glasses. The eye doctor asked Erick how he could see the blackboard in school. He wondered if Erick had to sit in the front of the room. God forbid. He liked the back of the room. Anyway, Erick replied, "Why do I have to see the blackboard? The teacher says everything she writes." Yup, that photographic mind at work. He went to school the next morning with his glasses and came home with some interesting observations. He was surprised that the floors in the school were "speckled" and that when you look at the trees you can see the individual leaves. Erick wore glasses for years, then contacts, and when corrective eye surgery became popular he was a prime candidate and has enjoyed being without glasses now for many years. As luck would have it, the eye surgeon was an alum of Erick's fraternity, so Erick was pretty comfortable the day of surgery after spending most of the night before sleepless and nervous.

Erick had one other surgery as a kid. When he was first learning to ride his bike, we gave our live-in sitter strict orders that he was not to jump the curb until he was more steady with the bike. She didn't listen to a lot of what we told her (let the kids watch TV too much and made them put their backs to the TV when she watched her "soaps"). Anyway, I got a call just as I was leaving work one day that Erick had fallen on his bike and hurt his arm. I rushed home, and took him to the emergency room. He had a very bad break requiring surgery.

Joon was in Indianapolis for a judo tournament. I called the Indianapolis Chamber of Commerce who put me through to the Judo venue, and someone went out on the mat and got Joon and brought him to the phone. I think this is the only time I felt there was an emergency that required me talking to Joon right away. Joon was already scheduled to leave Indianapolis the next day and could not get home any sooner. I just needed to talk with him and wanted him to know what was going on.

Mom came over to the hospital and sat with me while we awaited surgery. The live-in sitter was home with Sonja. Erick's surgery was delayed until almost 2:00 a.m. because the surgeon was busy reattaching 4 fingers on a man who had started falling off a ladder in his garage and grabbed the track the garage door rolls on and sliced off 4 of his fingers. The surgeon later told us that he once attached fingers onto a man who had been drunk and decided to pick up his rotary lawn mower to trim his hedge. Ouch!

Erick's break was very close to the growth plate, and the doctor was very concerned that it may affect further growth of that arm. Thankfully, that did not happen and Erick only has a scar from the surgery to show for the break. They put in a pin that protruded out of the skin and had to be removed later on. When we went back to the doctor on a follow-up checkup, he said that because of Erick's age (5th grade maybe?) they usually went back in the hospital to remove the pin. Erick didn't want to do that, so the doctor told him that removing the pin would be a little painful but only for a moment. Erick said, "Do it!" and had it removed in the doctor's office.

The only other break Erick had was a thin line fracture in his collarbone. It happened when he tripped over the cord of the remote control for the TV. When he was little and TV remotes first came out, they were not cordless. So, you would have a cord drapped across the room, so you could change the channel without getting up and going over to the TV. Erick just ran across the living room and tripped on the cord. There was no cast required, just a shoulder and arm sling to keep the shoulder immobilized for a few weeks.

Erick did a lot of traveling while growing up. He went to Korea and Germany with Joon. He went to a Rugby camp in San

Francisco, Bible Camp in Minnesota, to Washington D.C. for a youth Government trip, back to Washington on a college search visit with Joon, spring break in Santa Barbara where he and some buddies stayed with the aunt of one of the boys and had an overnight on an island offshore—National Park. He went on a H.S. Choir trip to New York, plus lots of family trips to Yellowstone, Hawaii, Washington D.C., Chicago, Disneyworld, Disneyland, Atlantic City, Las Vegas, Phoenix, Duluth, and Detroit.

Erick always liked being dressed up, or at least I think he did, from a young age. He and my dad would get dressed up for church (when we went to Willmar to visit mom and dad) and come out in suits and ties. When he was little we would have to change his clothes during eating if he got them too messy. He always seemed to want to look neat and spiffy. When he got into middle school and high school he wanted to shop the brand name stores and had a great eye for fashion. He took a modeling course, John Casablanca, in high school, and it gave him a lot of self confidence and fashion sense. He was never one to wear torn jeans or sneakers held together with duct tape like some of his buddies. In college I think it was also similar. In college we bought him his own tuxedo because there were so many occasions where he needed one that we were going broke renting them.

I remember one really fun shopping spree with Erick when we went to Abercrombie before going off to college. I didn't tell him the budget, and usually we were pretty conservative on how much we spent for clothing. However, I decided before we left that we would pretty much buy whatever he wanted unless it got totally out of control. He picked out 2-3 sweaters, a few shirts and a few slacks/jeans. Then he wondered which ones he could have, and I said, "All of them." Bet he wished he'd even picked out more. I'm sure he figured that once he picked out everything he wanted we would go through and decide which ones he really needed. Before we went to the store I had decided that I would let him buy whatever he wanted. I was smart enough not to tell him until we were ready to check out.

Erick was baptized at Oak Grove Lutheran Church and my sisters, Karen and Kathy, were his sponsors. He was confirmed at Normandale Lutheran Church.

Sonja was born in 1984, and we felt our family was now complete . . . daddy had his princess!! As with the boys, Sonja was born at Fairview Southdale Hospital . . . and now lives next door to the hospital in her condo. She was due February 4. However, on January 9 I stopped in the clinic for a checkup on my way to work. Just as I entered the doctor's waiting room, I realized my water had broken. This was a new experience for me as with both of the boys they had to break my water in the labor room at the hospital. I told the receptionist that my water broke and she said that probably I just had to go to the bathroom. I looked down and said that the fact that my boots were squishing with water and my pants were wet may mean more than going to the bathroom. Just then the doctor walked by the desk, and the nurse told him of my predicament. He told me to go home and wait for the pains to start and then go to the hospital. If no labor pains started by 6:00 p.m. he said to go into the hospital because he would have to induce labor. Well, nothing happened, so Joon took me to the hospital at 6:00 p.m. and they gave me a drug to induce labor.

Joon did not go into the delivery room with either of the boys. However, I convinced him to go along for the 3rd baby. Big mistake. It was the worst darn labor. During those last moments Joon said, "That darn girl is already causing trouble." He was sure it was a girl. I almost broke his hand squeezing it during those final pushes. In fact, I pushed so hard that my face was peppered for days with little broken blood vessels . . . looked like freckles. My shoulders were also so sore and weak from holding while pushing that I couldn't reach up to comb my hair.

The next day, a nurse poked her head in my room and said that my little girl was doing well even with her heart problems. I became hysterical. Nobody had mentioned that she had heart problems. What was this? Was she in danger? I was calmed down by the nursing supervisor who came in shortly. A few minutes later Jon's cardiologist, Dr. Singh, poked his head in the door to my room. I panicked at the sight of him. However, he said, "Word was out that the Chi's had a baby girl, so I stopped in to check her out. She appears fine and beautiful. Congratulations!!"

The grapevine must be pretty good in hospitals too. I had had all of our kids at Southdale Fairview. I guess they do keep track of their repeat moms. The other nurse had mistakenly thought I was the mom of a 13 pound baby girl who had been born to a diabetic mom. I guess 'cause I was the biggest mom she figured I had the biggest baby. Well, Sonja did not have any problems, but I sure was hopping mad at that nurse.

Sonja was baptized at Oak Grove Lutheran Church, as was Erick, and my sisters, Karen and Kathy were her sponsors also. She was confirmed by Normandale Lutheran Church with the Service held at Our Lady of Grace due to renovations at NLC at that time.

When Sonja was born we lived in a small story and a half home on Abbott Ave. in Edina. Her crib was put in Erick's room. When we moved to a house on 70th street, when Sonja was almost 2, they each got their own room.

Our house on Abbott had a detached garage on the alley. I remember when Sonja was about a year old she was standing in her crib in the window of her room and we were watching Joon shoveling tons of snow in order to get the car out of the garage. Well, he shoveled two paths from the garage out to the street so each set of tires would have a cleared path. However, from my vantage point next to Sonja it was obvious that the snow between the two paths was higher than the bottom of the car. I tried banging on the window to get Joon's attention and warn him that he needed to shovel more in the middle. I failed. He didn't hear me. He put the shovel aside, got in the car, put it in reverse, gunned the engine and flew backwards out of the garage. The car was all the way out of the garage before it got hung up on the snow he had left between the two paths. I turned to Sonja and said, "Confucius say snow easier to shovel when no car on top!" as Joon lay down on the snow to shovel the snow out from under the car. I don't think he ever did that again.

Sonja never had any surgeries and no major broken bones but her share of sprains and scratches. She's plagued with weak ankles and has used crutches a couple of times when she has sprained or otherwise injured her ankles.

I dressed her in frills and bows and lace when she was little, but as soon as she could pick out her own clothes and choose what to wear, that was the end of the fru-fru.

She went to college at a time when students wore flannel pajama pants and flip flops as regular fashion. She did dress up for school dances and parties, though. We bought a couple of her gowns at David's Bridal. One time we went when they were having a super sale. We found a dark burgundy satin gown that fit her perfectly. It was on the $99 rack. However, it had a snag in the fabric, so I asked the clerk if it could be marked down any further. She looked at the tag and said, "I don't think it could be marked down any further, its already $39." We tucked that puppy under our arm and headed for checkout. She had several other gowns over her high school and college years. The wonderful thing about Sonja was that if she really liked a dress she would actually wear it again. Not something every fashion conscious girl in Edina was willing to do. She didn't have to go to the name brand stores but always had good taste in what we did buy. It took me awhile to quit buying stuff without her along, though, as I wasn't very good at guessing what she would like.

Sonja and I made a tradition in high school to spend a day in the summer at the Mall of America. It usually meant some semi-uncontrolled shopping, lunch and a movie. It was a special time for us, and we still do it once in awhile. The outing is somewhat dimmed by my mobility. They do have rental electric carts at the Mall, but they are not very sturdy and run out of power after an hour or two, so we've had to switch for a different one partway through our day. One year we took my manual wheelchair, but most of the Mall is carpeted, and it was really hard for Sonja to push her pudda mother around. We still enjoy it.

Sonja also did a lot of traveling while growing up. She went with her middle school classmates to Washington D.C., the church choir to Texas and to the Pacific Northwest, the high school band to Disneyworld and other shorter trips. She was along on lots of family trips, same as Erick. She hasn't been to Germany or Korea, like Erick, but she spent January Term while at Luther taking a theatre class in England. She was not only able to see productions but get behind the scenes and learn more about the English theatre. The next school year her close friend Anna spent a year studying in England, so we sent Sonja back for a visit as a Christmas present that year so she could see Anna and enjoy more of England. She really loves England, and I am convinced she will be back there again for a visit.

She has also traveled to the Carolina's for a friend's wedding as well as Wisconsin and Iowa to see her friends. She and I made several trips over the years to visit my sister and her husband near Chicago. When she was in 8th or 9th grade and too young to drive and I got tired, we'd stop at a famous Wisconsin cheese house, and she would meander around while I took a 15 minute snooze in the car in the shade of a giant black and white cow structure outside the cheese house. Once she got her license, she did most of the driving. These trips were always a lot of fun, and we often planned them for times when Joon was going to be out of town for judo events, so we would be doing something fun too.

Our favorite stop on the way to Chicago was at the Lark Inn in Tomah, Wisconsin. It's a great motel, very old style where you park outside your motel room door. One time we brought along a laptop when Internet use was just new. Well, we dialed up, thinking an 800 number wouldn't cost any more than the usual local call charge. When we went to check out they had billed us $90 for Internet access. They knew us well there. We stayed at least once or twice each summer, and when I explained we weren't aware of how the charges were, they removed them. It turned out that there was really no cost to the Motel; it was just a charge that they billed guests for. They had a little snack bar where you got free breakfast, there was a gas station and a superette all in the Motel Office. They rented videos too. A real all-service place. We didn't have to stay overnight there, but we always did on the way to Chicago and usually drove straight through on the return trip. Tomah also had a great European style market for tourists and was a regional center for Wal Mart, so they had a fantastic Wal Mart store that we always stopped and visited. There is a great steakhouse downtown Tomah . . . nothing fancy, but great food. We have met my sister Karen and her husband in Tomah a couple of times and had lots of fun.

Sonja played the French horn in elementary school for just a couple of weeks. Good thing it was rented. She switched to the flute and became a very good musician. She learned to play other instruments in high school and college, but the flute was her major instrument. She took piano lessons for awhile, as did Erick, but neither of them were interested in continuing beyond the first year or so of lessons. That was fine. We liked to encourage them to try things. It is good to also have children follow through and finish what they start. But, if they really aren't interested in a hobby or pursuit, there's nothing wrong with cutting your losses and moving on!!

I enrolled both Erick and Sonja in Yamaha music courses at the Edina Community Center when they were pre-schoolers. It was something you did with your kids. They learned rhythm, notes and lots of things about music. They also learned to use an electric keyboard. It teaches a real appreciation of the fun of music, and I think it was very worthwhile for them. I would recommend it for all parents. Once the kids began instrumental lessons in the 5th grade, they already knew a quarter note from a half note and how to read musical notations. I'm sure this made it easier and quicker for them to get into actually learning the instrument. When we enrolled them in Yamaha we had also looked into Suzuki violin but realized that Suzuki was mainly just rote memorization, and Yamaha seemed like a much better choice.

Our kids are a joy to us, and we are so proud of them. We hope we did the best we could in raising them. It would be fun to be a mouse in the corner when they are with friends and talk about their parents. Then again, maybe not. We just know we are loved, and they know they are.

Chapter 6

Teaching Should Be an Olympic Sport

(13 Years as a High School Business Teacher)

When I was young there were very few role models for girls in our little town of 350 people. The only women professionals were school teachers. There was no hospital so no nurses. There wasn't any business in town that had a woman in a position of power. Several small business were run by husband and wife teams—two grocery stores, a restaurant, gas stations, etc. We had a beauty shop in the next town. There were a couple of women working at the bank and the post office. And, we had a switchboard operator who lived in the building where the switchboard was located. By the way, our telephone number was 7. And dad's business had the number 76. When you wanted to make a call she picked up and asked "Number please" in a nasal kind of voice then rang your call through. Country lines had 2-3 sharing a line, and when you listened to someone else's call you were called a rubber neck. The operator would ring a pattern of rings for various parties on the shared line so they knew who the call was for. If I came home from school and mom wasn't home, I could pick up the phone and ask the operator if she knew where my mom was. She would say, "She's over at Mae Olson's having coffee" or "She's at your Grandma Felt's house." Needless to say, she could listen to any and all conversations and probably did because she always knew everything going on in town.

Back to careers. I enjoyed cutting hair and giving perms. I even remember seeing a lady get a perm with the rods wired to heat—looked like something from outer space with all of them hooked up to her head. I also remember the odor of the ammonia or whatever chemical was in the perms being so strong that at the beauty shop sometimes our eyes would burn so that we would literally hang our head out the window to catch our breath. Well, I browsed the school library for beauty schools and decided I wanted to go to the beauty school in St. Cloud upon graduation from Cyrus High School.

My parents, however, were not excited about me going to beauty school. They wanted their girls all to go to college . . . REAL college, not beauty school. Dad said he couldn't figure out why anybody would want to stand and work in someone else's dirty head the rest of their life. I was a bit stubborn, and finally, dad sat me down and said that if I would go to Augsburg College, his alma mater, and take the 2-year secretarial degree program he would promise that when I finished the 2-year program they would pay for me to go to the St. Cloud beauty school. I was an excellent business student—loved typing, shorthand, accounting, etc. I agreed to go to Augsburg for 2 years. Once I got to Augsburg I realized that I really loved college, loved the business program and went right on for 4 years to get a teaching degree. Guess my dad figured that is probably what would happen if he got me to Augsburg. They had a great Business Department and a very good teacher education staff. I enjoyed the concert band while in college too. I guess I had found my path. I would stay on that path for 13 years.

In 1967, the year I graduated from Augsburg, there was a shortage of teachers. Principals from outstate Minnesota would contact Augsburg in the spring, go through files of seniors who would be graduating, and contact us. I received a call from Clarissa, Minnesota offering me a position as their Business Teacher. The school was so small they only had one Business Teacher. I said I would like to go to Clarissa and see the school before committing to a contract, so the Superintendent invited me to come up on the next Saturday. I toured the school, loved the little town and said yes. He handed me the contract and had me type it up at his Secretary's desk and put in the pay, $5,600 for the year, and had me sign it. So I walked down the aisle at graduation, knowing where I would be teaching in the fall.

Clarissa, Minnesota

Clarissa is a small town but bigger than the one I grew up in. There was a little creek ambling through the town which overflowed one year (July of 1972 I think) when we had an 8 inch rainfall. It brought the Governor to the city to look at the damage as some houses had their basements washed out from under them. The Governor at that time was Wendell Anderson, a former member of an Olympic Hockey Team. He was Governor until 1976 when he resigned to become U.S. Senator to replace Walter Mondale who had been elected Vice President of the U.S. Minnesota had two Vice President's that I recall . . . Hubert H. Humphrey and Walter Mondale. Needless to say having Governor Anderson visit Clarissa was pretty exciting.

When I first went to Clarissa, no band played a fanfare, no politician gave a speech, no press tore down the doors to get interviews with this new teacher. I was no celebrity, but to me it was an historical day. I walked proudly into my 1st hour class in my 3rd floor classroom of the 75 year-old structure and announced, "I'm Miss Tinseth and I'll be your typing teacher this year." On the outside I maybe appeared calm, but within my ample frame, my heart was pounding, and my knees felt like they would not support me. Just like in the movies, I wrote my name on the blackboard. I was not nervous; I was excited. My very own classroom! It was pretty exciting. This was truly the realization of a dream.

I said that this class was Typing I just in case any of them were in the wrong room. Sure enough, 3 freshmen sheepishly got up and left the room. Then I began to read the class list. Here is where you separate the Norwegians from the Bohemians. I read "Karjola, Knosolla, Aspengren, Reierson, Kuhne, Bican" with interruptions after almost every name correcting my pronunciation. Much to my relief, I soon came to Bill Johnson's name. Gave that boy an A!!

As each class filed in, every 50 minutes, the same routine followed. However, because of some siblings in subsequent classes I actually got some of the pronunciations correct. Things went well until Bookkeeping class when 55 students filed into a room that was set up for 18 students. So, I had them standing all along the sides and the back of the room, and a lot of chairs were shared by 2 students. The Principal was making rounds to see if there were problems. He sent about half of the students to study hall and later got some of them into Biology and had them take Bookkeeping the next semester. It all got ironed out, and he left me with about 25 students—more chairs and tables were added by the next day.

Roll call for Bookkeeping was pretty interesting. In this small town of 500, I had 3 sets of twins in one class! Trudy and Judy, Leland and Larry, Larry and Gary. They were all identical twins and all dressed exactly the same almost every single time you saw them in school or elsewhere. I never really could tell them apart and often wondered how many times they pulled a switch, just for the fun of it!

The last class of the day roll call went fine. However, when I got to the last two boys seated in the back I asked one of them how to spell his last name. Don't know what caused me to ask him, but somehow I had a feeling these two were up to something. He replied, spelling Reierson incorrectly. I said, "Maybe Knosolla would be easier for you to spell." They fessed up and said they were planning to confuse me from day one. They were fun kids and after that they seemed to realize that teachers have some kind of 6th sense. I found over the years that there were many schemes that flopped miserably because I was often a step ahead of them. However, I will never know how many schemes worked . . . only previous students would know that.

There is an old saying that "You can lead a horse to water, but you can't make him drink." But nobody said you can't put salt in his oats! Motivating students is where education begins and what it is all about. As in the case of the salty oats, the teacher must in some way make the students develop the thirst for knowledge. Self-motivation is the best possible kind of thirst, but much motivation in schools is also caused by peer pressure, parental pressure, and, of course, fear of failure when the report cards come out. So this motivation may be fear, need, inborn drive, curiosity, challenge, mystery, personal attachment or some other force. The force has to be there. And the more the force builds up out of the person himself, the more the person will learn of his own accord. I like to think that my sense of humor, leading by example, respect for students and other teachers, and genuine compassion for my students is why, I feel, I was pretty successful as a teacher. A teacher never really knows the impact they have on their students. However, through the years I am amazed at students who have either looked me up or who I have run into during the normal course of events who have told me of the positive influence I was in their lives. Those rewards are wonderful and mean a lot to me.

I would set attainable goals for my students and do everything I could to help them achieve them. I remember one time in particular when I was the student, and they were the teachers. It was a first year Accounting Class, and they just didn't seem to "get it." In exploring where they were having troubles, I discovered a pattern that indicated that maybe I had not gotten through to them. So a couple of weeks into the class, we stopped and started the class over. I told them I had failed the first test and to their surprise, admitted that it was me who needed to start over. We did, and all succeeded the second time around. I found this to be helpful as a manager in later life. If you make a mistake, admit it, correct it and go on. It fosters more respect than trying to alibi your way out of it. Or worse, yet, blaming someone else for your shortcomings.

Sometimes I would reward hard work with some comic relief that was actually more learning, but they just didn't always realize it. I would teach proper placement of addresses on envelopes in typing class and have them address letters to Ann Landers and actually make up a letter to Ann about a real or fictional problem. The letter had to be in the correct format, and they were graded. The most fun was that I would save the best ones and read them on the day before a vacation, or the day of huge snow storm when the kids were difficult to settle down, or a day when I felt they needed to be awakened. One letter to Ann Landers read:

March 25, 1968

Dear Ann,

Will you please help me. My problem is my typing teacher. Whenever we have a history test (and history is next hour) she loads on the work.

I'll admit she isn't as bad as our English teacher—nobody could be that bad. You know what? After I've typed this far I'm not mad at my typing teacher any more, I'm mad at my English teacher. Thanks for listening to me.

Yours truly,
Don

He even had the envelope properly addressed. And with the zip code, which was fairly new in those years.

On Valentine's Day I often had them compose poetry and put it in the proper typing format and fold it to make a Valentine card. I was always amazed at their ability to write simple poetry. They wrote their poems during the class period, so they couldn't go to the library or get outside help. Some were old familiar "Roses are red, Violets are blue . . ." but some were original. They didn't have to sign their names unless they wanted to . . . . and that is a bit risky I know. Here are a couple of samples I kept:

For Valentine's Day . . . . I am sending you a
"Thunderbird"
Really it is just a parrot I've been feeding
"Navy Beans"

and,

Roses are red
Violets are white
You would make one heck of a wife.

and,

Hi Valentine!
Just 3 little words . . . .
Just get lost! (and this one was signed!)

and finally,

Roses are red
Most plants are green,
You're one of my teachers
And the nicest I've seen!

Roses are red
Violets are blue,
As for my favorite teacher
I think I'll take you!

Roses are red
Third hour's the best,
But as for my poem
I think it's a mest!!

One poem I found sad was from Dave:

As I Look at Myself
No one understands me
No one even tries
No one really knows me
No one thinks I'm wise
No one finds me helpful
No one calls me bright
I know I'm not perfect
Maybe they are right.

The best creative poem, though, was from Debbie, not on Valentine's day. Debbie's mom was the English teacher.

Ode to a Typist

There she sits, pecking at keys
She's working so hard, her teacher to please,
The fingers get tired, the going gets tough,
She says to herself, "Boy I hate this stuff."
Then teacher comes by, with ruler in hand,
So the typist keeps on, how much more can she stand?
She smiles so sweetly as teacher goes by,
Then she grits her teeth and heaves a big sigh.
"27 hours straight, I've had enough."
She stand up and screams:
"This assignment's too tough!"
Then teacher comes over, the ruler comes down,
The typist is dead, she falls to the ground.
'Tis a sad ode, but true, true, true,
It happened to me, it could happen to you!!

Once in awhile I have asked students to tell me what grade they think they deserve. It is interesting that most of them are harder on themselves than I would be. In one particular typing class, only one student came back to say he deserved an A. Here is his note he typed:

Dear Miss Tinseth,

I thought I would write (and I use the word loosely) a letter and inform you that I deserve an "A" in this course.
Although I have yet to type twenty words a minute, I have been diligently trying to increase my typeing rate. So think kindly of me on judgement day.

Your studious pupil
Myron

and this student was hoping not to fail:

Dear Miss Tinseth,

I think that I should get a D because Im such a nice little boy. It isnt my fault I cant type I was born with club fingers.
Have to get after my mother and father for that. I just LOVE typing class with such a good teacher and to have such a well mannered boy in your class.
Thank you for your graces time to read a poor boys letter of pled.

Yours truly,
Jedd

and this one was a realist:

Dear Miss Tinseth:

I think that in this class I should be getting a 'C' or "C-' because I cannot keep my eyes off the keyboard. I also type too many errors for the number of words I type.

However, I will not complain at the grade I do get because I will know that it is what I deserve.

Sincerely,
Jan

Surroundings are important in creating an atmosphere conducive to learning. There are a number of ways to create the necessary atmosphere. The first and foremost item of importance is a teacher with a positive approach and a sense of humor, which I have mentioned before. You think this sounds simple? Not so!! How about the day . . .

- I was lecturing in front of an eager attentive class and caught my wrist watch on the back of my sweater and had to wriggle my hand out of it and let it hang there the remainder of the hour because the subject was too serious for comic relief.

- I walked into class on a beautiful spring day to find all of the windows flung wide open and nothing in sight but a long row of behinds as students hung their heads out the windows. After they all sat down, I reminded the students that the teacher is the only person allowed to open windows, walked over to the first window, slammed it shut and had closed it on my suit jacket!!

- One day I was showing the students the proper use of a paper cutter. I had a huge cutter with every marking and feature needed for cropping and cutting. This was not your ordinary paper cutter! I was standing at my desk, leaning over the cutter with my class crowded around my desk. As I was cutting near the top of the cutter, I didn't realize, until I was done and stood up straight, that I had cut off the end of my scarf that was hanging around my neck sort of like a tie.

- I was about to give a timed test in typing class and said "Hands in position, ready . . ." and hiccuped instead of saying "Begin".

- Or my sister who taught Home Economics was doing a unit on VD (now called STD) and telling her class that one of the symptoms was the inability to maintain one's balance. She turned around to get something out of the file cabinet by her desk, tripped on a floor outlet, and fell flat on her face.

Student involvement is also important. Real life exercises are important. Sometimes they go badly, however. While teaching the use of the telephone in a modern day office, I felt it was important to go into some detail as to the use of

DDD (Direct Distance Dialing). I like to refer to this now as Dumb Demands are Drastic. I told the class to put into practical use the simplicity of calling universal information and getting any listed telephone number on the United States mainland free of charge. Most of them were totally unaware that this was, at that time, a free service. The previous summer I had visited Washington, D.C. and had torn the page out of the hotel phone book that listed the number for the White House. So, the assignment was to get the number for the White House. They were to bring the number to class the next day. Out of a class of 23; 13 of them had successfully completed the assignment by getting the required number, 7 forgot to do the assignment, 2 didn't have telephones in their home (something I never thought about) and one spent 7 minutes talking to a mortuary in Texas. Fortunately, I wasn't asked to resign nor pay the long distance charges.

I also used role playing which also has the potential to get out of hand. A mock trial in the Business Law class got out of hand when a contract had to do with a farmer, his daughter, a salesman, and a bill for $10. Well you can guess this had to be nipped in the bud.

The use of Audio Visual equipment was helpful too. Equipment used then was a far cry from that found in today's media centers. We had film strips you turned manually in the projector and the text was written for the teacher to read or was on a record. We had movies, but projectors that were so temperamental you never could be sure you had a plan. Every school that I ever taught in had an AV "geek" who wheeled the equipment around, got out of lots of classes by doing so, and was often a little nerdy, but for sure was appreciated by the teachers. Clarissa's was Mike, and he was a wonder. He could make any piece of equipment work. He was always getting out of one class to assist a teacher in another. He helped with school pictures when the photographer spent the day to take pictures for the annual (now called the yearbook). He seemed to be everywhere at once. I often wonder what he does now and how it may be related to his experience in school.

I wasn't ever a Principal, but one note that a 7th grader brought in when he was late for school read:

To Mr. Kamrud,

Yesterday my brother and I went out in the woods and found some red berries. We each ate some. When we got home mom said they were poisonous so we were waiting to get sick.

Dad

and,

Floyd was late for school 'cause he was chasing the dog!

One other interesting experience was the "Daily Bulletin" which was brought to each classroom and read by the teacher. It came at the end of 1st hour so it showed attendance and tardiness for the day, plus announcements. Sometimes what they said was funny, and sometimes the typos made an ordinary notice funny.

- High School Teachers: Please return the films and records for the 'Studing for Success' series to the library as soon as you finish.

- The baton class will not twirl Friday night.

- Toilet behaviour: Please keep both the boys and girls lavatories clean. It is reported that there has been some misuse of the toilets in the girls room. Let's be careful what we do.

- As the weather warms up and you need the windows open, make sure the windows are open only 12" or less.

There were thoughts of the day:

- "Yesterday is a canceled check; tomorrow is a promissory note; today is the only cash you have; spend it wisely.

- "The man who makes no mistakes usually does not make anything."

- "Poise is the art of raising the eyebrows instead of the roof."

Now these are the types of quotes we see making the rounds on the Internet.

Something else in schools in the 70's was having proms in the school gym. The gym was transformed into a magical place where any resemblance to a gymnasium was removed by the addition of tons and tons of crepe paper streamers strung over the entire ceiling and sides on wires strung carefully across and around the huge rooms. In Clarissa, all 12 grades were in the same building and shared many areas. Something that happened in Clarissa was the elementary principal who also taught elementary phy ed went into the gym, and turned the key that lowered a curtain to divide the two ends of the gym so two separate classes could be held at the same time. Of course, this brought down all of the wires as well as any crepe paper that had already been strung by the shop teacher and his students. Dear Mr. Nygren! After the first time he did it we had a "Nygren lookout" when decorating began, so we could stop him before he did any damage. One year someone had the bright idea to have a water fall/fountain. Well, it leaked (predictable) and a part of the costly hardwood gym floor had to be replaced. Teachers all helped with after school activities, and prom was no exception. The faculty all attended and women teachers wore formal gowns.

It was a fun few years in Clarissa. I directed the church choir in the Methodist church and one of the Lutheran churches. As was the case in many small towns in Minnesota at that time, there was one Norwegian Lutheran Church and one with Swedish roots. There was also a large Catholic church and a couple of other small denominations. I loved music, and my background in church and school choirs helped me a lot. My years in instrumental music in high school and college also gave me good musical background. I played the piano but not well. But I loved to sing. Of course the choirs in both churches sang a lot of the same songs. Neither choir had gowns, but when a church elsewhere bought new gowns, we got the old ones for free, and I used some of them at each church. The choirs were both small with only a dozen or so faithful members in each of them. A favorite song of mine was "Wonderful Grace of Jesus" an old hymn I had learned that was a favorite of my mom's when she was growing up. It has a fantastic chorus that lets the men shine, and it is my all-time favorite.

The first year in Clarissa I roomed with Marilyn who taught special ed. She was a nice person, and we got along well. She had one bad habit—she bit her toenails when she sat on the couch and watched TV. We rented a very small 2-bedroom house across the street from the school. The closet between the two bedrooms opened to both so was sort of a walk-in I guess. There was no basement and a tiny kitchen. The stove was an old, old style with the oven to the right of the burners and counter high. The stove was open below and had curvy long legs. It had a lot of character but didn't work very well as I remember.

When Marilyn got married and her new husband was home from the military service, I stayed with the Mellenkamps on their farm for a couple of weeks. Mrs. Mellenkamp was also a teacher at the school, so I knew her well. Before school I would go gopher trapping with her husband. She was a great cook, so we ate well. Each morning she brought out the same black iron frying pan and fried bacon and eggs, in the same leftover fat from the previous day(s). It sounds gross, but it sure tasted good. I really enjoyed the stay on the farm.

I went fishing with the Hayes family a few times. They were next door neighbors at the time. Once we were casting off shore for northerns using perch as bait. My rod and reel separated from one another when I hooked a fish, and I ran up the hill from the lake hollering "I got one, I got one." People came running to see what the heck was going on just as a huge northern flopped onto shore.

My sister Karen joined me my second year in Clarissa. We rented a house for awhile, then later bought a 3-bedroom mobile home and put it on a lot of our dear friends Leo and Ramona Hayes. One Sunday we came home from church and opened the door to the house and were met with billows of black smoke. We had put a roast in the oven before we went to church. We had just bought a new stove and found that it had a bad thermostat, so it just kept getting hotter and hotter until the roast literally burned up. I went in the kitchen, grabbed the potholders and threw the burned up roast, with pan to match, into a snowbank. By then the fire department showed up because neighbors saw the smoke. Well, needless to say my sister took a lot of teasing about burning the roast, her being the Home Ec teacher. There was so much smoke that we had to wash or dry clean all of our clothes and had a real mess. Also, when we opened the kitchen door Karen's dog flashed past us like a bolt of lightening . . . no doubt scared to death and wanting some fresh air!

The house had a basement and a ping pong table, and I remember enjoying playing gnip-gnop as we called it. The house was owned by the Mayor of Clarissa named Dixon. It was painted pink and on the edge of town. We should have bought that house, but instead we bought the mobile home. Dad advised us to buy the house, which would appreciate in value, but for some reason we insisted on buying the trailer house, which depreciates in value.

The nice thing about our trailer was that it was not in a trailer park, but on a full lot in a neighborhood, and it faced the street. Dad and mom spent a weekend with us, and dad, with our help, built a large deck on the front of the trailer which was very nice. Rather than pay rent for the lot, the Hayes' said that if we paid to bring water/sewer and electricity to the lot we could live there rent free, and the improvements to their lot would be adequate compensation. We loved living next door to them and were dear friends for years.

We bought a snowmobile and had a lot of fun those winters. When the temp fell to -50 degrees, our furnace went out during the night, and we awoke to 47 degrees in the house. We called the gas company, and they said that propane could be carried in an open bucket in those temperatures, so it was not feeding through the pipes into the house. They told us to take a bucket of warm water and pour it on the propane tank in the back yard and it would bring the temp up enough so gas would feed through the line, and we could re-light the furnace. We put on our snowmobile suits, went out with the bucket of water, went back in and lit the furnace, and finally hopped on our snowmobile and went downtown to the Do Drop Inn (the only restaurant in town) and spent a few hours drinking coffee, eating and playing cards while the house warmed up.

The Do Drop Inn (honest, that was the name of it) had the best thousand island dressing I have ever had. When I was about to leave town, they gave me the recipe . . . . mayo, tons of paprika, sweet pickle relish and ketchup. It was something about the combination and amounts, but it was fantastic. Right across from the Do Drop Inn was Bican's meat market. In those days we got cow tongue, tail and heart free from the Bican's because so many people butchered their own cattle that they couldn't get rid of those items. To this day I think of the free cow tail when I pay $3+ a pound for ox tail to make soup. One day someone knocked on the Home Ec room door in the middle of class and delivered a big bag of Rocky Mountain Oysters to my sister. Cute, very cute!!

The first place I lived in Clarissa was at Anderson's. It was the 2nd floor of a story and a half. I couldn't stand up straight, but almost. There was a stove and frig, but the only sink was in the ½ bath which meant sink and stool. The shower was in the basement through the breezeway from the garage. It was clean, and it was nice, and it was cheap. It was also furnished which was great for Marilyn and I just starting out. One night I came home from playing cards with some friends who lived just outside of town. While we were playing, there was an ice storm we were unaware of. Well, it was so slippery we formed a human bridge from the back door of their house to the cars and helped one another try to stand up. I think I only had to drive a mile or two and crept along to stay out of ditches and away from trees. However, when I got home, it was so slick that when I slowly put on the brakes to pull over and park on the side of the road, I slid into the lawn, landing just outside the kitchen window. I left the darn car there and was able to walk to the house on the crunchy/icy grass instead of the sidewalk and didn't fall.

When I started teaching in Clarissa none of the women teachers wore slacks. I don't recall if we were not allowed to wear slacks. It was probably just something women didn't do at that time. Anyway by the mid 70's we were into polyester pants suits and no more nylons and garters. Panty hose arrived, and we were thrilled. Of course, I could never buy mine in a normal store . . . had to order by mail from the Lane Bryant fat girl store in Minneapolis. When researching my notes for this book, I came across a copy of a letter I wrote to Roaman's (fat girl catalogue) in New York inquiring about starting a Roaman's store in Willmar where my parents lived at the time. I don't recall if I ever got a response. Probably not. I loved to dream about doing all kinds of things.

I was teaching Economics in Clarissa too and at that time my dad had sold his realty business in Willmar. He opened a "big board" in an office downtown where people could exchange directly with the Chicago Board of Trade. Futures trading was exciting and you could lose your shirt as quickly as you could make a bundle. I really got interested when my class studied it in Economics, and I was trying to teach it and understand it. At my dad's office men would come in and sit down and watch the board click prices at the same time they changed in Chicago. Dad enjoyed it but didn't trade much himself. He had one huge investor who spent most every day watching the "big board" and traded contracts so large they could often see the price changes on the "big board" when he bought and sold. Tragedy struck one morning when the man was killed on the way into town when his car was hit by a train. Dad had to immediately pull this man out of all of his transactions, and the results on the "big board" were very obvious.

I decided to cash in a small insurance policy and play with it on futures. Dad's philosophy was never to invest money you couldn't afford to lose, and I figured the $2K was something I never realized I had until he told me and it might just go well. Lost the whole $2K. Never did any trading in the market after that. Never told the students I lost the whole chunk of dough.

One year we had a foreign exchange student from Ethiopia. Oh, my gosh. Many people in town had never seen a black person, much less a foreigner. I will never forget one of the first days of the school year when the choir director burst into the teacher's lounge and exclaimed, "I can't believe it, he (the Ethiopian student) can't sing and has absolutely no rhythm. Unbelievable!!!" He was a wonderful kid, and we got along well. In fact, he came back after graduation and attended my alma mater, Augsburg College, much to do with my influence he told me. He stayed with a nice farm family named the Behrends. They had a great family, and we got to be good friends.

Clarissa had a local newspaper, *The Clarissa Independent*. It had all of the usual news and had a local news item, gossip column, that appeared every week. Dee, the social page reporter, would call and instead of "hello" she would say "Have you any news?" The column told who visited whom, who had coffee, who visited from out of town, and on and on. Needless to say the teachers tried to stay out of her column.

And then for teachers there were "other duties as assigned." This meant lots of things to my sister and I in Clarissa. We sewed and glued 25 emblems and letters on letterman jackets for the jocks one year; we took tickets and made popcorn and hot dogs to sell at sporting events; I supervised the school paper and the yearbook; Karen supervised the cheerleaders and even sewed uniforms for them. One summer she and I drove to The International Peace Garden on the North Dakota and Canadian Border and took the cheerleaders to a cheerleading camp. We stayed on the Canadian side but drove back to see them every day. Plus, brought prune juice for one of the gals who was constipated beyond belief.

After graduation, two of our students got married so my sister and I helped them with the wedding plans, made bridesmaid dresses and helped paint the inside of the run down farmhouse they were to move into. One Saturday we were out on the farm painting the interior and being goofy. We decided to paint a couple of nasty words on the wall which gave us a good laugh. I said, "This is about when the preacher pulls into the yard." Not 5 minutes later the preacher drove into the yard. Some quick whips with the roller covered the words, but somehow, we couldn't believe our brush with the clerical collar!!

Some prices in the mid 70's: class play matinee for elementary students was 10 cents each, yearbooks were $4, rent for me was $300 a month, my car payment was $50, and $20 bought a lot of groceries, not just one small bag. Students were released from school once a week for religious instruction. Kids were excused for deer hunting. Students paid 25 cents to ride the spectator's bus to away ball games. Teachers chaperoned on a rotating schedule. If there weren't enough students signed up for a spectator's bus, the cheerleaders would ride on the player's bus, and there would be no spectator's bus. Senior pictures were taken by a photographer who came to the school and set up in the Home Economics room. Every once in awhile the school would designate a "dress up" day. The students would come in their Sunday best and behavior was always better on those days. Teachers loved dress up days, but probably parents didn't appreciate them so much as this community was not wealthy, and some students probably didn't have much to dress up in.

Each church in town held special services for graduates much like they do now. At the Lutheran Church they held a joint graduation and confirmation service because they had a small church and there were usually 8-10 graduates and about the same number of confirmands. One year I spoke at their service, and one year I played a trumpet duet with one of my students.

When I began paying back my Government student loan and gave my address as Clarissa in Todd County, I received a response stating that 10% or 15% (can't remember exactly) would be forgiven each year because I was teaching in a designated poverty county. This was a pleasant surprise. Then when I left in 1973 to go and teach for the Department of Defense Overseas, I was notified that the rest of my loan would be forgiven for doing Government Service. So, I never had to pay back my college loans—totally without knowing what I was doing. Dumb luck.

The years in Clarissa were great years. I made lots of wonderful friends and will always remember those first years of teaching as being very special. I taught there from August of 1967 to May of 1973

Busan, Korea

In August of 1973 I began teaching in Busan, Korea. It was on Hialeah Compound, an Army Base. I was a civilian employee with the Department of Defense.

My roommates in Busan the 1st year were Lynda and Jonnette. Jonnette was pretty interesting. She was the Home Economics teacher and loved to cook and entertain (in more ways than one). She would turn the kitchen of our 3-bedroom rambler in the Bachelor Officer's Quarters (BOQ) into a total disaster, but the food was good, and we were always included just because we lived there. The down side was that we never knew who would be in her bedroom when we got up in the morning. Our house was popular with the single officers on post, but Lynda and I were not the cause of it.

Lynda was a good Mormon from Utah, and she and I became lifelong friends. Our lifestyles were similar, and we enjoyed many of the same things. There were Mormon Missionaries in Busan who she met through the Mormon Church that she attended off post. One time we had several teachers over to our house, and she introduced the Missionaries as Brother Aldan and Brother Paul. Allan, a teacher in attendance, actually said, "Wow, they both have the same first name." The sad part is he was not being funny. Lynda explained it to him. Poor Allan.

Ordering from a menu that is totally in Korean had it's challenges while I was in Busan. The first week I was in Korea I went with several other teachers to a small hole-in-the wall Chinese Cafe in Busan. Most larger restaurants had menus in English or staff that spoke some English. This little cafe had neither. After agonizing about how and what to order we finally started drawing pictures. We drew a chicken, and they seemed to understand what we meant, so we ordered a dish that we thought would have chicken. Then we drew a cow to get some beef dish. When they served the food, they put down what we thought was beef, and we tried to verify what it was. Deep in our minds we were concerned about getting dog, which we had heard was eaten in Korea. We don't know what the meat was, but it tasted great, and we enjoyed our evening out.

One time four of us went to a fancy downtown Korean Restaurant. It was a husband a wife, Kathy and Leonard, me, and a friend Don, the math teacher. Well, we took our shoes off at the bottom of an open curved stairway that led to the elegant second floor. Our shoes were taken out of sight and brought back when we descended the steps when we finished dining. Well, they had put my shoes next to the shoes of Leonard, the large Polish husband and his wife's tiny shoes were next to the math teachers shoes that were smaller.

The longest phrase I learned in Korea was "you go, I'll stay home" which is about 3 times as long in Korean. Little did I know that that phrase would apply to me many times over my 35 plus years of marriage as my husband is a world traveler for his love of Judo, and because I don't like to fly, I have seldom traveled with him. However, I have always supported his travels because it is something he loves, and it makes him happy. He has no other vices—doesn't smoke, drink in excess, chase women, hunt, fish, or have any vices so it has been easy to support him in something that is so good . . . amateur athletics. He has been a Judo referee for most of our married life. He has traveled all over the world for the sport and eventually officiated at the Olympics in Sydney. He is now a Commissioner for the PanAmerican Judo Union (PJU) which consists of 42 countries in North America, Central America, South America and the Caribbean. In 2008 he was honored by the PJU by being inducted into the Judo Hall of Fame; an honor that he is very proud to have received.

When I packed to go to Korea I tried to take all of the creature comforts with me. I packed a waffle iron, and it made me very popular with lots of people on base. Living on the base was carefree. Nobody had to do their own laundry or cleaning or home maintenance, so we had nothing but spare time once our lesson plans were done and papers corrected and graded. We'd also have donut making parties. It was fun to get together and do "back home" stuff.

Lynda and I liked to go to the Officer's Club and play pool in the bar on Saturday mornings before the bar flies showed up.

Lots of weekends we'd have sightseeing excursions together with other teachers. We traveled and explored Korea whenever we could. The GI's didn't seem to be as adventurous. One time we asked a GI to go with us off post to eat "on the economy". He had been in Korea over a year and it was the first time he had gone off post to eat.

Teaching had its challenges as included in Chapter 1. Besides the small size of classes, supplies were very limited. We didn't have the latest textbooks, but we had enough to do a good job. I've never worked with a more professional and dedicated group of teachers. No slackers, nobody just collecting a paycheck.

The second school year began with tragedy. One teacher who had arrived a week early was found dead in his BOQ. They found out later that he had advanced stages of cancer and probably was aware of it. The tragic part of the story is that when he fell ill they contacted a Base doctor who finished his tennis game before checking on the call and in the meantime the fellow died. The doctor disappeared (was transferred we later found out), and we never got any more firm information on what had actually happened to cause the sudden death of the teacher.

Another teacher was only in Korea a few days. When her household goods shipment arrived from Baharain, a stash of pot was found. She was whisked out of the country quickly and never heard from again. Other than these two incidents, there wasn't anything too exciting that happened.

I made lots of friends in those 2 short school years who I have kept in touch with ever since. One interesting character was Bill Sharpe. Bill was a large man . . . bigger around than me. He was older and was a good friend. He had a girlfriend off post, as did lots of GI's and a few teachers. I was privileged to have him take me along to meet her on one occasion. She had a darling little toddler running around who looked a lot like Bill, but I never asked. She was a nice person and I was glad to meet her. Our Principal was married to a Korean lady and they lived on Base. He drove a red pickup with a covered back . . . Bill called it the "red bed." He had been in Korea many years before someone snagged him and got married. Probably he was a popular bachelor 'cause he was a great guy and good looking.

The principal had a sense of humor too. If there was space available in the school, foreigners living in Korea as well as affluent Koreans could pay tuition and enroll their children in schools on Base. When the wealthy Korean or Japanese parents would come in to pay their tuition, in cash, he would bow to them time after time after time because they would bow again each time he bowed. Those of us who happened to be sitting in the office having our before school cup of coffee tried to keep from bursting out in laughter. He did it in such a way that it didn't seem like he was really making fun of them, just of the tradition.

The school had a fax machine, but the type of paper made it important to get copies made quickly because the fax would fade for awhile until finally it disappeared. There was no fancy copier or other modern office equipment that I was used to in the States.

Drugs were a problem with a small number of our students. I found out after I left there that one student was actually mainlining heroin in the school bathroom. The fact that most of the students were children of officers made discipline fairly easy. If their kids caused trouble, the officers got in trouble, so things were usually dealt with in a fast and efficient manner.

Although Busan only had snow once the two years I lived there, we had lots of cold weather in the winter. Once in awhile there would be temperatures low enough to put a thin glaze of ice over puddles, but rarely did they stay frozen once the sun came out. The climate was pretty moderate compared to what I was used to. Each quansit hut, one for English, one for Business, one for Math, etc. had its own heating unit, kinda like the ceiling ones I'd seen in garages in the States. So, we were dripping with sweat until October when the weather turned cold, and then we froze until spring which came in March. I taught many classes in my coat and sometimes with my gloves on. But, it was a way of life, and we just accepted it, and nobody really complained all that much.

In our BOQ's (Bachelor Officer Quarters) they came around one day and put metal boxes over our thermostats, so we couldn't turn them up for more heat. The boxes had holes drilled in them, so the temperature of the room would register on the thermostat. They were set at 68 degrees which is pretty cool when you are sitting around in the evening and all of the floors are linoleum, not carpet. Well, we used to hang a plastic bag full of ice cubes over and around the box, so it would fool the thermostat into thinking it was even colder than 68 degrees. This worked pretty well. The base maintenance people also put rat traps in our houses. They were huge—the rats and the traps! One day we saw a huge rat go up the wall in the kitchen, but that was the only time I saw one the whole time I was in Korea.

Although our BOQ's were fairly sparse we didn't complain. No rent, no utilities, no complaints. The one thing I missed was a bathtub. All of the BOQ's had showers only. The Officer's Quarters, located in another part of the base, were side-by-side duplexes, and they had fireplaces, and they also had bathtubs. A couple of times a friend, whose husband was an officer, invited me to her house for the evening just so I could take a long soaking bath. What a luxury that was.

One other thing I missed in Korea was fresh milk. I never bought milk off the base, and the milk in the commissary (base grocery) was reconstituted. This meant that it had been frozen or dried or something. Anyway, it was not very good, and the first Christmas when I went home to Minnesota for the holidays I drank so much ice cold milk and took so many hot, soaking baths that I lost count.

Besides teaching, I did get involved in a couple of other pursuits while there. Jon Blom and I recorded reel to reel tapes of English textbooks for the Busan Public School District. I think there may be Koreans still there with a bit of a Norwegian twist to their English. I played piano/organ duets with Jon for graduation too. Graduation was held in the Base Chapel. I remember taking our house maid to a Korean eye doctor and buying her glasses because she couldn't afford them. We helped the Korean economy by doing lots of shopping. I was asked by the Principal in Taegu's American School to go there to help them set up a business work program for them. I went to teacher meetings in Japan. I went on my first and last blind date when I was there at Yokota AFB. I'm a 6'1" robust

Norwegian, and as you can guess, if this guy was 5'5" he was lying!!!! However, after we got over how short he was and how tall I was we actually had a great evening and I did not regret the experience. We talked for hours and enjoyed each other's company.

The only resource materials I had in Korea were what I had brought with me. Each teacher traveled with their own files and materials. Unlike when I taught in the U.S. There were no cupboards or file cabinets full of materials to thumb through to use or get ideas. I'm glad I brought lots of stuff with me. Actually, some teaching supplies and materials are still in a couple of boxes in my garage . . . just couldn't toss them, but they are all so outdated they could never be used in the classroom today.

I taught for two school years in Korea, from the fall of 1973 to the spring of 1975.

Farmington, Minnesota

The road to Farmington began in San Francisco. In the spring of 1975 we decided to move back to the States. Joon wanted to finish college, and we wanted to start a family. Joon was 30 when we got married and I was 29. In Korea it is tough for half and half kids, AmerAsians, to get along. They are treated badly and often the product of GI's lovin' and leavin' them behind. I resigned my position and we prepared to move to the U.S.

In June, along with some teacher friends we all planned an overnight together in San Francisco before we each flew our separate ways home. We all stayed at the same hotel and had a nice time. However, Joon wasn't feeling very good and rode the cable car with hardly a comment. The next day, we hopped a plane for Los Angeles to meet up with my two sisters who had flown there to meet us. We were all at our Uncle Lloyd's. Well, Joon's indigestion kept getting worse, and finally, we took him to the Emergency Room at the local hospital in Ontario, California. He had to have emergency surgery for a burst appendix. He was in the hospital quite a few days, and recovery was slow. His incision drained for months, but we were just glad he survived. He was very sick.

102 Phyllis Dianna Tinseth Chi

Karen and Kathy had flown to L.A. with the plan that the 4 of us would drive home to Minnesota together and get to know each other. Uncle Lloyd had found us a station wagon, at our request, that we could drive home in. Well, Joon would not be able to travel for at least a month, so Karen and Kathy took off in our car and headed for Minnesota. In the middle of July, Joon and I flew to Minneapolis and were met by family who delivered our car to the airport, so we could drive to Willmar ourselves. Joon was in the back of the wagon on soft pillows and blankets. I decided to give the Augsburg Teacher Placement Office a call before heading out for Willmar and ask them if they had any job openings from schools in the Twin Cities area as we wanted to be in a location where Joon could attend college and I could get a teaching job. I had updated my credentials via mail in the spring so I would be ready to apply for jobs as soon as we got to Minnesota. The Augsburg Placement Office said that they had received a call that morning from Farmington High School, and they were looking for a Vocational Business Ed Teacher. I called Farmington, told the Principal that I had flown in that morning and could I stop by for an interview that afternoon. He said ok, so I swung by Augsburg and picked up my packet of credentials to bring it along to the interview. Normally this is mailed to the school prior to interviews, but they made an exception and actually let me pick it up. At that time we were not allowed to see our credentials, which contained confidential recommendations from former bosses and co-workers. Anyway, they sealed it in an envelope and let me hand carry it to Farmington.

Joon was resting comfortably in the back of the station wagon as we drove to the southern suburb of Farmington. The interview went well, and afterwards, we headed for Willmar. A few days later I got a phone call offering me the job in Farmington. So, we found a small apartment just off Nicollet and 98th Street in Bloomington, Joon enrolled in Normandale College and we moved on.

I found out later that there were over 200 applicants for the job at Farmington. Times had changed since college graduation when everyone was pretty much guaranteed jobs because of the shortage of teachers. I also found out in

August that I was pregnant, something I didn't know when I applied and interviewed for the job. Needless to say I was pretty concerned about telling the Principal that I was actually pregnant when I was interviewed and would need maternity leave in late February. Jon was due February 24 but didn't arrive until March 8, 1976. Although my faculty peers were happy for me, the Principal's attitude toward me changed, and I felt that he was holding it against me. However, after he got to know me better and saw my skills in the classroom he warmed up again, and we got along very well the rest of the time I was in Farmington.

The first day of teacher orientation brought all of the teachers in the District to the high school for meetings. I'm walking down the hall and I hear this voice behind me yelling, "Phinna", which is the nickname I had all through grade school and high school, but left behind when I went to Augsburg. It was Jim, my closest male friend from high school. He was teaching in the elementary school. I was so surprised, as was he. Next, I met a H.S. teacher who was the son of a pastor who was in our small town when I was growing up. It is a small world. I met lots of wonderful people in Farmington while I taught there, even though we never lived there.

Because I taught in a vocational setting, I had students working at the bakery, the FAA air control center, a bank, a pallet company, a factory in Lakeville and many more locations. I had to find the jobs, which meant visiting numerous businesses. Then I had to supervise the students at their jobs. My sister Karen was now head of food service at a nursing home in Apple Valley. They hired one of my students to help the social workers and residents open up a small gift shop in the lobby. We set up the bookkeeping system, and the student worked directly with the staff and residents to make the gift shop happen. The most interesting place for me to visit was the air traffic control center. The main room was filled with green screens bleeping with locations of aircraft—just like in the movies.

I worked with one of the math teachers, and we taught Fortran computer programming to his math class. I always was fascinated with computer capabilities and back when I was in Clarissa I convinced the Superintendent that all students should be required to take a semester of typing, so they would be better prepared for the future growing technology. Hey, sometimes I'm right!

Like every school I taught in there were teachers who dazzled me with their expertise . . . and those who were collecting a check and didn't care about their students at all. I felt I fell somewhere in the middle. I cared about my students a lot. Often, I was able to get some of the "problem" students focused in something they could succeed in and by giving them more attention turned some around who were definitely headed for trouble. This was true in Farmington too. A few years later one of these students who was nothing but trouble all through school stopped to see me at the HUD office in downtown Minneapolis where I went after leaving Farmington. He was now a successful businessman and credited me with helping him go in that direction. One of those rewards I've mentioned before. Another student from Farmington was my teacher aide her senior year. For over 20 years after graduation she and I exchanged Christmas cards. However, I've not heard from her for the past couple of years but still send her a card in the hopes someone will respond. I hope she is ok, but I haven't been able to find her or get her to respond.

I don't have a lot of vivid memories from Farmington like I did for Clarissa and Busan. My focus, once Jon was born, was literally to keep him alive. I have areas of time that I recall almost nothing. I didn't keep a folder of "book ideas" in my lower right hand drawer; something I had done in Clarissa and Busan and had continued to do in all of my years working for the Government. I think that it is because of the stress of having a child so ill. I would often leave work and drive directly to Children's Hospital to deal with Jon's latest crisis. Weekends were often spent at the hospital. I think I still devoted myself to my students, but once I drove away at the end of the school day, my focus was totally on my home and family, more than ever.

Chapter 7

There is Life After Teaching

(My Career with the Federal Government)

In the spring of 1980 I was teaching Vocational Office Education at Farmington High School in Farmington, Minnesota. To assist students in finding jobs in business upon graduation, I decided to take a bus of students to the Federal Building at Fort Snelling to take the Civil Service Test, which was a requirement at that time to get into Government Civilian jobs. I had textbooks that had chapters on the Civil Service Test, but I had never seen the actual test. So, when we got to Ft. Snelling I spoke with the lady from OPM (Office of Personnel Management, the Personnel office for the Government) and asked her if it would be okay for me to take the test even though I had no intention of seeking a Government job, just wanted to take the test to make me a better teacher. She said that would be fine. She said to put down a salary requirement high enough so nobody would call me regarding an office job. I assume she thought I would do well on the test, and I should as I had been teaching business for 13 years and thought I was pretty good, actually.

Well, I took the test, and for the salary requirement I put down the salary I was getting at the time as a teacher with 13 years of experience, which was just over $13,000 a year.

We bounced back to Farmington on the bus and went on with our business studies. We finished the school year and none of the students had yet heard from OPM regarding their test scores or available positions. Well, in June, I received a call from the Department of Housing and Urban Development State Office asking if I would be interested in a Clerk/Steno position in their office in Edina (which is where I lived) which was moving to downtown Minneapolis in a few months. I said that I wouldn't be able to take a job with a cut in pay, which I was sure would be the case, as the job was a Clerk/Steno, (Grade) GS4, Step 1, which paid less than what I was getting as a teacher. However, Marla, the Personnel Specialist who called me said that because of my 2 years as a Civil Servant in Korea at the GS9 and GS11, they could go up in steps to a GS4, Step 10, which was about $50 less per year than I was making teaching! In the Government, the lowest jobs are GS1's and go to GS14's on the general pay schedule. Within each grade there are 10 steps. The grades are determined by the position and amount of responsibility as outlined in the job description. If I recall correctly, within each grade, there are 10 steps that increase one step per year until you reach a certain level, then you have to wait 2 years between step increases. Well, she was not able to give me a higher grade but could go as high as the 10th step, the limit within the GS4, in order to try and match my previous government salary.

My husband and I had some very serious discussions about this job offer. I was commuting 40 miles to Farmington, our son Jon was in and out of the hospital frequently and I was spending a lot of time on the road commuting, going back to take on other teaching responsibilities at the time which included taking tickets at sporting events, supervising dances and the whole array of "other duties as assigned." We finally agreed that at this time in our lives this change would fit in well with our personal needs. We decided I would ask for a leave of absence and do it for a year and see how I like it.

I agonized about sending a letter to the Board of Education asking for a leave of absence but had to give it a try. I mailed my letter on a Monday morning. In the mail on Tuesday I received a letter from the Farmington School District. It couldn't be a response so quickly. I opened the letter and to my astonishment, it was a letter informing me that my position had been cut to part time due to budget cuts and me being the newest hire on a staff of 4 in the Business Department. This would also have been a cut in pay, something I could not afford with mounting medical bills at home. I called the Superintendent at Farmington after reading the letter, and we talked about his relief and mine. Our letters had crossed in the mail . . . he was feeling bad to cut me to part time and I was feeling bad about asking for a leave of absence when I had only been there a couple of years. Well, they granted me the leave of absence and as you know by now I never did go back to teaching. My legacy at Farmington is that I was hired there to start the Office Education Program which is a vocational state subsidized program that allows students to work afternoons in office jobs while getting credit in the business program. I accomplished that before I left and it was thriving. For this I felt a feeling of accomplishment and pride.

So, it was off to HUD. After a year as a clerk/steno I applied for a Support Services Supervisor (SSS) position and was selected as a GS5. The position went to a GS9. You have to be in the grade a year before being promoted, and I received the promotion annually until I was a GS9. At that point, I had to make a change in position or remain a GS9 forever. As SSS I was responsible for Health and Safety, Security, vehicles, the mail room, stock/supply room, copiers, as well as overseeing all facilities management and purchasing for the Office.

The head of Management wanted to get me into his Division as a GS11/12. However, he told me privately that the head of Administration (my boss) and the head of the Office would never let me get promoted because I did such a good job as Support Services Supervisor that they didn't want to let me go. He told me that if I ever wanted a promotion I would have to go to another Government Agency.

The part of my position at HUD that I enjoyed the most and wanted to continue doing was facilities management, including space planning and design. It just happened that a friend who worked at Fort Snelling in GSA (General Services Administration) Telecommunications and who I worked with frequently for phone installations, changes and problems, called me to say that the Immigration and Naturalization Service (INS) was posting a GS9/11 Space Management Specialist position in their Administration Division. I filled out an application and mailed it off to the INS. I received a call from the INS a few weeks later with a job offer, site unseen, over the phone. I said that I would like to at least meet the boss and see the office space before accepting. So, I went out for the interview at my request, accepted the job and went to the INS in August as a GS9 Space Management Specialist. There was no increase in pay, called a "lateral" because it was the same grade I already had. However, just not having to pay the high price of parking in downtown Minneapolis was like a raise to me.

So, in 1987 I went to the INS. I was a GS9 for the required year, then promoted to a GS11. A couple of years later the position was upgraded to a GS12, and I was promoted again. Our staff grew and they created a Facilities Management Supervisor to be the Chief of the Facilities Management Branch including 4 Realty Specialists, a Motor Vehicle Clerk, Safety and Health Officer, Property Specialist, and two clerks. I stayed in that position until 1999 when my boss, Ray, retired. When he left I applied for his position as head of Administration and was selected and promoted to Assistant Director of Administration at GS14, the highest grade I would occupy for the Federal Government. I had 3 branches in my Division—Facilities Management, Procurement and Support Services. I maintained this position with the INS until the establishment of the Department of Homeland Security (DHS) after 9/11. In the new organization my position was eliminated as our office would become a National Hiring Center for DHS with no facilities management except for our immediate office. They created a Human Resource Manager Position, GS13, for me, so I did not have to move to Dallas or some other location. I retained my pay but going to the GS13 meant no more raises or steps. I was just glad to have a job but did not like my loss of responsibility and the dissolving of our office as we knew it. A new boss was put in place who often wondered what I did for a living and never treated me as the competent professional I had been for many years. So, almost as soon as I was eligible, I retired and left the office, remembering the fun, exciting, stressful glory days of the old INS that I enjoyed even though the work was always challenging and tough.

One evening, after a grueling day at the office (really!!) with 3-4 executives from the Immigration and Naturalization Service Head Office in Washington, D.C. we decided to all go out to dinner at a local steakhouse. It ended up being 3 men from Washington, 3 realty specialists from my staff and a contracting officer, Ken, from my staff. Ken was seated to my left and suddenly stood up and waved his arms. I stood immediately and asked him if he was okay, and he shook his head "NO". I hadn't had a first aid refresher course or recertification for at least 10 years, yet without hesitation I asked him if he could speak, and he again shook his head "NO". I am 6'1", and he is about the same height as me. I put my arms around him and did a somewhat wimpy Heimlich maneuver. He did not speak and nothing came out of his mouth. Without a second thought. I gave another Heimlich with everything I had and a chunk of steak popped out of his mouth onto the table.

The other men at the table remained seated and speechless as they watched us. None of them even stood up, I think too stunned to react. We discussed it later, and I was the only one at the table who had ever learned the Heimlich or had First Aid Training, for that matter. After collecting our thoughts, Ken and I sat back down at the table. What do you do after you've just saved someone's life, and what does he do when he realizes how close he was to death? Nobody really said much; I picked up my fork and thought I'd just finish eating only to find that my hands were shaking so much that there was no way I could get anything on my fork, much less get it to my mouth. I quietly put my fork down and put my hands in my lap. I looked over at Ken and he was also sitting with his hands in his lap. I never asked him, but my guess is he was shaking as much as I was.

On my way home from the restaurant it really hit me. I had actually saved someone's life. It was a very strange feeling. Like, wow, I really did it. While relating the incident to my husband when I got home, I realized that it was even difficult to tell someone something so deeply emotional and actually sort of private, in a way.

Ken and I talked about it the next day at the office, and he said the reality of what had almost happened really hit him when he tucked his children into bed the previous night . . . that if it hadn't been for me, he may have never done that again. A few weeks later he gave me a very personal and passionate thank you card and also a small crystal guardian angel charm which I still have hanging on my bedside lamp.

I'm big, kinda unsure on my feet and use a cane, but none of that mattered when Ken needed help. My height and large size, I think, helped me in being able to succeed in the Heimlich. If I were 5'5" and 110 lbs. I often wonder if Ken would be here today.

Ken and I had another connection. In 1987, we both came on board at the INS as new hires. He as a contracting officer and me as a space management specialist. In 1999 I became the Division Director of Administration, and Ken was on my staff as a contracting officer until shortly before I retired in 2005. We had another connection. We both grew up in rural Minnesota and shared lots of memories over the years, especially Ole and Lena (ethnic Norwegian) jokes. In fact, as I write this, I recall that I sent Ken a new Ole joke on the Internet this morning. And, we both love pie!!! We often shared a break in my office with a great piece of pie and good conversation.

After the "Heimlich" incident, there was joking around the office that people wanted to sit next to me at potluck lunches in case anyone would need assistance. We had an annual office-wide pot luck at Christmastime, later called the Holiday Party. Ken was always trying to bring unusual dishes, and one year I think it was Ken who floated sardines in blue jello to make it look like an aquarium I guess. Pretty fun stuff.

The office potluck is an institution that I believe still thrives in most offices today. At INS there was one man who always brought a huge platter of rolled up lefse, a Scandinavian treat that is very labor intensive to make and loved by anyone Norwegian or Swedish, plus some converts. My husband thinks it is like eating your napkin—no flavor I guess. But if you smother it with butter and load it with sugar before you roll it up, it is pretty darn good.

Another memorable potluck item was a homemade rum cake which someone brought to our Admin office party which we often held monthly to celebrate birthdays. You know, when you cook or bake with alcohol most of the alcohol dissipates. However, this cake had the rum added and soaked into the cake after it was baked and before it was frosted. I'm not sure how much productivity there was in the office that afternoon, but I know several staff who had more than one helping! I actually peeked into the conference room in the afternoon and not only was the cake gone, but the plate looked like it was licked clean. A year later the INS Employee Association put out a cookbook, and the rum cake recipe was in it. Come to find out there was only about a tablespoon of rum in the whole cake.

The head of the office, Stan, loved the potluck parties. We think it was because the food was free. Stan was someone who stayed very close to his money. He would go to a training class at a fancy hotel and bring his brown bag lunch and eat it on a sofa in the lobby. His staff assistant, Gene, once said, "If you are walking with Stan and he sees a penny on the ground, he will pick it up. If he sees a quarter, get out of his way, so you don't get hurt as he dives for it!" Stan also took "casual Friday" to new lows. He had a sport coat hanging in his office in case a big shot showed up from Headquarters, but he never wore a suit in the office as the previous Director had. His casual style of dress trickled down throughout the office. Sloppy sweatshirts, jeans, sneakers, anything was okay. Yet, some of the staff, including me, continued to wear office attire, and some of the men wore sport shirts and ties with dress slacks. Prior to retiring, my boss, Ray Brown, wore a suit and tie every day. He was a rare and dying breed of professionally dressed managers in our office. On casual Fridays Stan would wear sweat pants and t-shirts. In the summer, he would wear running shorts.

I recall one time when Stan was going to travel to Washington, D.C. on business. My husband was a supervisor at the airport and they were overbooked on Stan's flight, so they upgraded a couple of people to first class. Stan could have been upgraded to first class, but one look at Stan in his running shorts and lettered t-shirt sealed his destiny to stay in the back of the plane. And liquor in first class is free. Stan never knew what he missed that day.

There were some other interesting incidents that happened when I traveled for the government. On one flight to Washington D.C., my husband paid for me to be upgraded to first class where there is more room for my long legs and large body. I was seated and comfortable in first class sipping a soda when they began boarding the rest of the passengers. As I sat there, the head of the office, at that time, walked past me in the aisle on his way to the back of the plane.

On another occasion another head of the office (there were 5 different Directors during the years I was at that office) and I were both on a flight to Washington, but he did not see me as I was seated in an aisle way in the back, and I saw him get on the plane, but he was many rows ahead of me. Again the flight was overbooked, and they offered cash bonuses for anyone who would get off and take a later flight. I didn't offer as I had a meeting scheduled and didn't want to be late or miss it. The head of the office at that time took the offer. I reviewed his travel voucher when he submitted it for reimbursement and saw nothing on it to indicate he had taken the cash bonus and a later flight. Interesting.

I went to Chicago on business many times over the years as the project that I think was instrumental in "launching my career," as it is often stated, was moving the Chicago District Office of the INS from the Federal Building in downtown Chicago to a 10 story office building nearby. The office occupied the entire building, and the project was mine to handle from looking at prospective buildings, through planning and design, to actual move-in, a process that took about 2 ½ years. We toured a lot of locations before settling on a building very close to the Federal Building. It was on Jackson Street.

The person the Chicago Office Director had assigned to coordinate the move with the Regional Office, me, was a real pill. He used to work in Headquarters in Washington, D.C., then was transferred to the Regional Office where I worked, and when he fell out of grace there was transferred to the Chicago District Office. The joke in the office was that eventually he would end up on the Northern Border in a one-man border station.

One huge dispute I had with Chicago was that their coordinator wanted the investigators to have systems furniture within their private offices. We had designed the space giving them private offices. Then, while designing the furniture layouts he wanted 84" high systems furniture panes within the offices space. By using systems/modular furniture within private offices, we were doubling the furniture costs. By building them private offices and then putting in 84" panels, we would literally be putting walls within walls. In an office the size of the Chicago District, we're talking about a waste of a huge chunk of change. When I wouldn't budge on the private office issue, I picked up the phone one day and a woman's voice said, "Please hold the line for Mr. Moyer." He was the head of the office and had never called me personally or directly before that day. He asked me about the office for Investigator's issue, and I explained that we had planned for one type of office and by adding the 84" panels and making the change now, during construction, we would be wasting a lot of taxpayer's money. The cost of the office walls was built into the terms of the lease. The 84" panels within the walls were an additional cost and served no real purpose. We were more than doubling the cost of those offices if I agreed to their demands. As I told him, "This is the kind of stuff newspaper headlines love." He realized his coordinator was giving him erroneous information. He thanked me for the information and hung up. I never heard another word about the 84" panels. Suddenly, I had a new point of contact in the Chicago Office. The coordinator must have been taken off the project as I never spoke with him again, and rumor was that he was "put on a shelf" in Chicago—drawing a paycheck but not really doing anything. This is how his whole career went. He was ex-military and said he would retire once his military and civil service retirement totaled $100k per year. He retired a few years later, so he probably made his goal. Personally a fun guy to talk with and be around but not easy to work with.

On one trip to Chicago, I got in a cab at the airport, and the name on the license in the cab and the speech of the driver indicated to me that he was Korean. So, when we got to the office building in downtown Chicago, I thanked him in Korean.

He was surprised and asked me how I knew Korean. I told him my husband was Korean, and he asked his name. I told him, and then I said, "He's the Mr. Chi who is very well known in Judo." He replied that he indeed knew who my husband was. Well, he wanted to know when I would be done at the office and he would be there to take me to the hotel. He was my private chauffeur for the 2 days I was in Chicago. I still paid him, of course, but he was always at the curb when I had said I would need a cab. What a pleasant trip.

On one trip to the Detroit office I called the principal of the high school I taught in while in Korea to say I was in town. He had retired, I thought, and lived in Detroit. He came down to the office, and we had lunch together and talked of the wonderful times in Korea. That was the last time I saw him. He gave the bride away at the Korean wedding ceremony we had in Seoul. He was a wonderful principal and person. At least that is what I thought. He was caught with his "hand in the till". In other words, when foreign students came to our school on the military base and paid him in cash, he allegedly skimmed some off the top for years and finally got caught. None of us on the staff were aware of this, or at least I don't think so. He eventually got caught and was sent back to the U.S. He was not put in jail but had to repay the amount, and I believe he was on probation. Well, the IRS ended up putting him in prison to serve time for tax evasion as he did not pay taxes on the embezzled money. After he served his time, he got a job as a public school teacher. On his application he had admitted that he was a convicted felon, but apparently no one had noticed it, and he was hired. Part way through the year someone was going through the files for some unrelated reason and noticed that he was a convicted felon, and he was let go. The last I heard he was selling real estate, I believe. I am very saddened to have lost touch with him and his wife and son. Regardless of what he did, I considered him a good principal and close friend.

In one position I held, I received reports from the Veteran's Administration (VA) Blood Bank telling of employees who had donated blood. Our office policy, to encourage blood donors to give, was to allow 4 hours of paid Administrative Leave for the purpose of blood donations. Time to travel to the VA hospital, donate the blood, rest and drink your orange juice and eat the cookies they provide, and get back to the office or home. The usual routine for employees was to go after lunch and then go home after leaving the VA. The head of the office had no problem with this. Well, some people will always push the envelope. One day, while reviewing the latest printout from the VA regarding blood donors, I was sitting across from the secretary who reviewed all the Time and Attendance sheets (called T&A's, honest!!!) before they were submitted for payroll. She said, "Oh, I see Dan's secretary gave blood again last week." I had the VA report in my hand so looked at it and said, "Yup, she was there last Thursday." Cindy said, "No, on her T&A it says she took Admin leave on Friday after lunch." Somehow we decided to check, so I called the VA to confirm that she gave blood on Friday as her T&A stated. The person there looked it up and said, "No, we don't do donations on Friday, but she was here Thursday night as we are open until 8:00 p.m. She was here in the evening, I'm sure." Well, we had to report this to our boss, then she spoke to the secretary's boss and she was put on unpaid leave for 3 days for her "creative" blood donating schedule. The rumor was that she was taking the Administrative leave on Friday afternoons and leaving at noon to head for wherever her boyfriend was attending college. She was donating blood Thursday night AFTER work hours. This had been going on for sometime. Everywhere I have worked there have been people like her who push the rules to their limit, and beyond, and wonder why they get in trouble. She absolutely saw nothing wrong with what she was doing because she WAS giving blood and we WERE allowed 4 hours to do so. Don't know how she figures the two could be disconnected.

For all of the years I worked for the Government, I spent tax payer's money as if it was my own. When I was the head of Facilities Management in the INS Regional Office, there were 4 Regions. Each Region had to prepare their annual budget request. I always made sure that ours was realistic and honest. We did not pad it with useless numbers in order to get more money. We asked for what we truly felt we needed. This paid off big time. The Western Region was known for asking for the moon as far as funds were concerned, but they never had the documentation to show how or why they needed the funds. The Eastern Region was well run, but they were known for building the Taj Mahal when the rest of us were being reasonable in our requests. People from our Region would visit offices in the Eastern Region and find them to be lush and plush. The Southern Region in Dallas was known for being disorganized and also got in some trouble for buying items with Government funds that should not have been purchased as they were upgrades from what was really needed. So this brings us back to us, the Northern Region. One of my staff often padded his requests for funds for the projects he was in charge of. You had to be a bit generous because there were often costs that came up during a project that could not have been foreseen. However, this employee was the king of padding. When I challenged him he got really angry at me. I finally spoke with him and told him I didn't care what his opinion was regarding padding numbers. We were only going to ask for funds that we legitimately need and no "pie in the sky" kind of stuff. I held firm on this all the years I worked at that position. The reward? When we would get towards the end of the Government's fiscal year, Headquarters would often contact us first to say that they had funds available due to projects that were behind schedule or were scratched. They would ask us if we could use any funds and what we would use them for. We always had projects that had come up during the year or projects that through no fault of ours were coming in over budget. I know that we were treated well and included in many serious budget discussions because we were trusted and respected.

I had a great idea regarding the housing of Immigration Inspectors on the remote sites along the Northern border of the U.S. We provided housing for the Inspectors, but there were a lot of run down houses out there that had not been maintained very well over the years. We began an aggressive program to try and bring these homes to a more comfortable situation for our employees. I think we owned 38 houses; Customs owned some, and we each took care of our own although some of our people were living in Customs housing and some of their's were in our housing.

We replaced appliances as we could afford to do so, and because for many of them it was up to 100 miles to a full service grocery store, we also bought small deep freezers for their convenience. We also felt that they should be responsible for maintaining their property as tenants do. With no leases in place there were no rules about maintaining the property. These employees paid rent to the Government by way of payroll deduction. The rents were very low, but they did have to pay it. Some paid their own utilities, and where meters were shared by the Port of Entry buildings and the housing, they were billed for a reasonable amount. We provided and maintained emergency generators at these remote locations also.

After we sent out leases for current tenants, I received a couple of funny phone calls. Both calls regarded the phrase in the lease that they were to "leave the property in the condition that they found it." First, an Immigration Inspector called and said that his daughter had been going through a wild phase and "got herself pregnant." And, he had put up walls in the basement to make her a bedroom and playroom for the "kid" cause the "man that got her in trouble ran off." His question was, "Do I have to remove those walls when I move out?" We told him it was ok to leave them.

The second call was from an Immigration Inspector who had been in a remote site in Montana for many, many years. He said, "I read your lease, and I only have one comment. My wife and I discussed it and don't think we can get the weeds to grow as high in the yard as they were when we moved in!!!" Then he laughed and laughed. For the most part, we got a lot of compliments from people in INS housing that they at least felt we were paying attention to their needs and doing what we could to make them more comfortable.

As a Government employee for so many years, I saw so many dedicated employees who were responsible and dedicated. They put in a full day's work for a full day's pay and truly cared about their jobs, their co-workers and their Country. It was an honor and a privilege to work for the Government. I felt that I was doing my small part to help.

On the other hand, there were a few real clinkers that I met and worked with over the years. I had one outspoken lady who forever spoke before thinking. One day she hung her boobs over the transaction counter of a secretary's desk area next to an openly gay employee. At that moment the mail clerk handed out the CFC (Combined Federal Campaign) brochure outlining what causes we could designate our charitable giving for in the next year. This is the Government's "United Way." She grabbed the brochure, thumbed through it and commented in a very sarcastic tone, "Well, I wonder what gay and lesbian groups we can donate to THIS year?" I went into my office and asked her to join me. I sat her down and really let her have it. It took a lot to get me truly angry at an employee, but her history of tactless remarks and disparaging remarks finally went over the line. I spent a lot of time in my office, with the door closed, counseling her on appropriate remarks and how to get along in the workplace. Finally, I was finished, and she agreed that she would try to do better. She stood up, opened the door, and before walking out she turned to me and said, "Wow, you are not nearly the wimp I thought you were!!!" She was relieved from her job shortly thereafter.

In Administrative Services we handled the day-to-day support of problems in the building. For example, employees contacted us about problems with phones, copiers, heat, cold, clogged toilets, parking, etc. You name it, and if an employee had a concern, they contacted us. Every spring we got complaint after complaint about the building being too warm. In a huge office building you don't simply turn a thermostat up or down at will. As we explained to employees each spring and each fall, the entire heating and air conditioning system had to be converted from one to the other. It didn't matter, people still complained each spring about needing air conditioning and each fall about needing heating. It was simple, GSA (who ran our building—we were just one tenant) turned on the heat about October 15 each year and the air conditioning in April or May. It didn't matter how much we complained; they had to make the best decision they could based on "usual" weather conditions. No matter, the complaints came every year.

There was one lady who felt it her duty to let us know about every possible thing affecting employees. She complained in the summer because she would ride her motorcycle to work, and if it was really hot, her kick stand would sink into the asphalt in the parking lot. She wanted us to put in a concrete area for bikes. She complained about the Federal Protective Service employees who took care of building security. She accused them of inappropriate touching when they scanned people upon entry in the front lobby. She complained about her office space (cube) and pretty much everything else around her. We implemented a procedure for complaints so that employees could send e-mail messages to "Administrative Services," and we could follow up with legitimate complaints and track correction of problems. She was our most prolific subscriber. It got to be fun just waiting for her next complaint. If the flag in front of the building was at half mast, she would want to know why. If there was a death and she felt the flag should be at half mast and it wasn't, she'd contact us about that too. We had no control over the flying of the flag in front of the building. It was controlled by the Federal Protective Service (FPS) in Washington, D.C., and the local FPS would receive a notification from them and could not make a local decision on the matter of the flag. We told her that numerous times, but she still continued to contact us at her whim.

One e-mail complaint from Ken H. read "The water appears to be off colored. It was noticed in several bathroom stools and urinals today by different people. Is this a problem GSA is aware of? It appears that the water would not be drinkable." I responded "Even if the color of the water is not 'off' you shouldn't be drinking from the stools and urinals ever!!" He enjoyed the response, and we both laughed. We were sensitive to the needs of the employees and most of them were realistic in their expectations, and we appreciated being able to make their work life better.

The first employee I ever fired was a young man, just out of high school, who was bright, fun, talented and should have been a long term great employee. However, he started calling in with "basketball" injuries from his club he belonged to and also seemed to have a lot of visitors at his desk from other agencies in the building. His work started to fail. He was the teletype operator, something INS used until the mid 80's. He was to finish all teletypes each day because they were only used for urgent business. One day he had left early, saying his teletypes were done for the day. He had to take vacation time or no pay for leaving early, but he had a basketball game. Anyway, after he left someone asked about a teletype that should have been sent. There was no record of it. When I searched his work station, I found the teletype that had not been sent, along with several more that hadn't been sent all hidden under his "out" basket. When questioned about it he admitted that he had done it and had done it before. About that time the FPS (Federal Protective Service) was looking into some concerns that there may have been some drug dealings going on between our employee and others with other agencies. I never heard that the allegations were substantiated. To make a long story short, I had to fire him, and the FPS escorted him out of the building which was standard procedure for anyone fired in the building.

There was another employee who "on the sneak" would skip her afternoon coffee break and leave 15 minutes early by scooting down the stairwell and out the back door of the building. It didn't last too long, though, as other employees ratted on her, and I finally witnessed her slipping out. She was able to find work elsewhere.

We had a purchasing agent whose son "borrowed" her Government credit card and treated his girlfriend to a weekend at the local Fantasy Suites for her birthday. Of course, upon reviewing the monthly statements we discovered his purchase, and she was reprimanded. She was a single mom and had lots of trouble with her two teenage children, and this was just one problem she had to deal with. We had a purchasing agent in Detroit who used his credit card to buy appliances for his home and electronic equipment that could be easily fenced. He actually served time in prison for his creative purchasing in the name of the Government.

In 1997 the flooding of the Red River in North Dakota and Western Minnesota threatened our Border Patrol location in Grand Forks. We sent one of our purchasing agents to the area with a van full of supplies (water, generator, etc.). We also rented a couple of RV's for them to work out of until their office could be dried out and cleaned. Any crisis in our 20-state region became our crisis. It was a busy but exciting time.

We had a small seasonal border station on the Northern Border that was in a mountainous area, and we routinely hired a company to plow the snow and open the road in mid-June for the summer. This was a station that was only open during the summer tourist season.

Once when I was acting in charge of Administration, the head of contracting, George, was hiring a new Purchasing Agent. He was interviewing the secretary for the head of Administration. The lady was very sarcastic, outspoken and tough to get along with. I couldn't imagine he would want to hire her. He came to me with the form to fill out because he had to recommend hiring her, and I had to sign to concur. I asked him why he would want to hire someone with such a caustic personality because she had a reputation for being difficult to get along with. He insisted, so I gave in. Later, after she was hired, I found out that she was a very close personal friend of the Contracting Officer's wife. She was sometimes difficult to work with, but ended up doing a very good job and going up in the ranks of the INS. Sometimes I'm wrong.

Sometimes hiring was a nightmare. It really is difficult to know who to hire, and the interviews are as tough on the person doing the interviewing as the one being interviewed. I hired a lady once who came to work on a Monday and never came back again. She told someone later that she was so overwhelmed by the work that she couldn't come back.

I hired several disabled American Vets and also a young lady who was legally blind. She came in under a special program to temporarily hire handicapped individuals. We had a great experience. We got computer software that spoke to her and worked with staff to determine what things would be best suited to her abilities. She found her place and was productive, and we were sorry when the time limit on the Program ended and she had to quit. However, I worked with her, and she was able to find a permanent job with another Federal Agency, so we had benefited from her work with us and she had been able to get work experience that enhanced her chances of moving on to another job. There were some who were hired and grew into the jobs and did great. Some came in hitting the ground running and never slowed down. It was all an adventure, and the greatest satisfaction was to help any and all of them succeed . . . just like it was to help students succeed when I was a teacher. I guess teaching and managing were extremely similar. They are just different ages, and paychecks replaced report cards. Maybe that is why I encountered many great managers over the years and they were often former teachers, like me.

Chapter 8

The Little Wedding That Grew

(Our Son's Marriage to Amy Adams)

Erick had lots of dates in high school and was a very social being. However, nobody stood out, in our minds, as being the "one for him." The most serious dating was his senior year and when they graduated she went on to play the field, and Erick went to the University not much interested, from what we could tell, in getting together with any particular gal. Well, that all changed when one night at a fraternity fund raiser he descended the open staircase at the fraternity house to be sold at a charity auction for a date. A lovely gal named Amy was there with a friend who was in a sorority that had been invited to the auction. She told us later that when he came down the staircase she said to her friend that that was the guy she was going to marry. She was struck by him; his coy act as he descended the staircase I guess. Anyway, later in the evening word got back to him about her comment, and he went over to her and said he thought they should be introduced if they planned to be married. The rest, as they say, is history. She didn't buy him for the date, but she got him for life!

In all of his college years this is the first girl that Erick brought home to meet the parents. He put it this way, "I'm dating a girl who I would like you to meet." With Erick's history of keeping his social life pretty private, we figured this must be "the one." Yup, she was. Joon had always said that it is easier to get along with people who are not picky eaters. Well, the first time Amy came to our house to meet us, we prepared a Korean meal, and she tried and seemed to like everything. Anyway, Erick cornered his dad in the kitchen and said, "See, I told you she's not a picky eater." We've chuckled about that ever since. She is a wonderful girl and feels like a true daughter to us. Shopping with her the first time was just like shopping with Sonja, spending carefully and keeping an eye open for a bargain. Anyway, we all hit it off well, and we couldn't be more thrilled that Erick and Amy found one another. Soon we met her parents and her brother and again, the apple did not fall far from the tree. They are all wonderful people and we hold them near and dear to our hearts.

It wasn't long after meeting Amy that Erick called us and wanted us to join him in a shopping trip to jewelry stores to look at rings. So on a horribly cold and snowy Minnesota winter evening, we met him for dinner and went to the HUB jewelers in Richfield to look at rings. He did not order a ring that night but made a decision on what kind he would buy. Thirty some years ago, in Korea, Joon had given me a platinum wedding ring in traditional Korean style with an almost flawless nice sized stone. We decided to give Erick the diamond from that ring to keep it in the family, and we would replace it with a fake diamond, so I could still wear it on special occasions. I had since received a full 1K diamond, so I'm still good with the bling. Anyway, Erick had the stone put in a lovely ring for Amy and gave it to her embedded in the back pages of a book he made about their courtship. When she turned the last page of pictures and remembrances, there was a hole carved in the pages with the ring nestled inside. Prior to that, he had done the romantic thing and had called her parents to make a date to go over to their house. His purpose was to ask for her hand in marriage. I'm so proud that he did such a traditional and gentlemanly thing. I imagine he was a bundle of nerves. Her mom and dad told us that they figured that was what he was up to. Maybe they were more nervous than he was. From everything

I can see, they are as pleased to have Erick in their family as we are to have Amy in ours.

Remember, I told Joon to replace the diamond in my Korean ring with a cubic zerconia, but of course, he simply bought me another diamond to replace the original that now belongs to Amy.

Erick married his bride in June of 2004. We had heard so many stories about the costs of weddings, we were determined to keep things from getting out of hand. Ya, right. How many times have you heard that? We were caught up in the excitement and hopped on the train that raced toward that wonderful day. I think when all of the receipts were counted up that we shared the costs pretty equally with the bride's parents. Our original thought was to spend $5K on our share of the wedding and have $5K to give the kids when they would buy their first house. So much for that thought. We exceeded all of that and don't regret a penny of it!!

The guest list was limited to 250 of their closest friends and relatives. A manageable size. However, when you multiply things by 250, it does add up. I had this great idea for favors for the reception . . . a simple little white box like the ones a velvet ring box is often enclosed in from a jeweler. It was simple, just use a hot glue gun and put white lace trim around the cover, put their name and date of the wedding on the cover, fill it with candy wrapped in tulle, and tie it with a satin bow. They were great. However, by time the items were all purchased and multiplied by 250, the cost was so much I still haven't told my husband how much they cost. If he reads this book, he'll learn that they cost almost over $2 each. Remember to multiply by 250. I even got a bargain on the little white jewelry boxes by visiting the jewelry counter at Wal Mart to see if they would order the boxes. They said they could not but that every time they ordered jewelry they got about 50-75 boxes, and they would set some aside for me. It is good that I plan things waaaaay ahead because I had to go back to Wal Mart 5 times before I had the number of boxes needed. Paying for the boxes became problematic. The computer didn't know how to ring up the boxes as they aren't ever sold, but given to the consumer when they buy the jewelry. Because I wasn't buying any jewelry, they couldn't give me the boxes free. The manager stepped in with a wonderful idea. They gave me the boxes free, and I gave them a check each time for the Children's Miracle Network, a charity they sponsor and so do I. One of those times when everybody wins! I worked on the boxes for awhile, and Amy's mom offered to take them over and finish them. She came up with the plan for how to get their name and date on the cover, and the joint effort resulted in some wonderful table favors. Given the effort put forth for this one item I'm wondering if those guests who left them untouched on the table had any idea? Oh, well.

My other creative contribution to their wedding day was volunteering, along with my husband's sister, to construct the bridesmaid's dresses. Five satin gowns in candy apple red, each a different pattern, didn't sound like all that much work. The task was way more than I figured, but I have this history of biting off more than I can chew and usually making it happen. Armed with a bolt of the precious cloth, the patterns that the bride and her maids had chosen, I put scissor to fabric and began working on the gowns in January. Did I mention that my sister-in-law lives in Los Angeles? Well, I cut out the gowns and then my husband flew to L.A. with the pieces to 4 of the gowns in a suitcase. She did the first sewing, then sent them back and I did the fitting and made adjustments and sewed the 5th gown here. The week before the wedding my sister-in-law flew in from L.A., and all of the bridesmaids converged on our house, and the day of final adjustments became like Hell week at the Citadel. Of course some had lost weight, some had had too much time to think about their gowns and wanted to change the straps, or the style. I had made a big mistake by telling the gals that because we were making them ourselves we could make adjustments to the patterns pretty easily. I forgot to emphasize that that had to be decided on *before* the dresses were cut out, not 3 days before the wedding at the final fitting. All but one of the bridesmaids got it . . . . the other one was just a pain. Because of her demands and changes she was the only one whose gown didn't fit her the best and looked like it had been put together by a committee. I did my daughter's dress because my husband's two sisters disagreed with Sonja and I on the style, so I had to do that one all by myself, and it fit Sonja beautifully, was very flattering for her body style and she and I were both happy with it. Somehow we got the dresses done, but there were a couple of nights that I sewed until 3 a.m. The sisters were two hours late for the final fitting day, so the bridesmaids were at my house waiting until we finally proceeded, and I finished up with everything myself. The two had decided to go and have eyebrow tattoos and of course it took longer than planned. Because my in-laws had volunteered to prepare a Korean feast for the groom's dinner, my sister-in-law was pulled out of sewing and went to cooking. I survived.

The groom's dinner included the wedding party and several out-of-town guests (and out-of-country). My husband's sisters, sisters-in-law and niece fixed a Korean feast that was fantastic and served buffet style. The highlight of the evening was the traditional bowing ceremony where the newlyweds bow to the groom's family—and not all at once, but by family unit. The bride and groom practiced bowing before the day to do it properly. They were outfitted in their traditional Korean dress for the occasion. They had had the Korean outfits custom made on a trip to Los Angeles with my husband months before the wedding. This was also a chance to introduce the bride to the Los Angeles branch of the Chi family. My mom attended the groom's dinner, but both of my sisters declined.

Back to the bowing. After bowing to the groom's parents, and groom's aunts and uncles, etc., each recipient of the bow presented the groom with an envelope of money for their wedding/honeymoon expenses which is Korean tradition. When they bowed to me and my husband I had Amy, the bride, hold out the skirt of her dress just as I had done in Korea 30 years before with Joon's mother, and I threw the dried nuts and fruits that I had saved all those years into Amy's skirt. I still can't believe I kept track of that little sack of nuts and fruit for 30 years as we moved many, many times, and as you will see in a later chapter, I was not known for my housekeeping skills while I was working full time, and we were raising the kids. The symbolism of the fruits and nuts is fertility related. When the bowing was done one of my son's male friends joked with him about wearing his "silk pink pants" and asked when he would wear them again. Erick joked back, waving many envelopes of money in the air, "I guess whenever I need more of this."

We Americanized the ceremony to include bowing to Amy's parents. As you may have guessed, or already knew, the male is definitely dominant in Korea. We all agreed on including them, and it was especially meaningful because she has such wonderful parents and a fantastic brother, and we wanted them to become a part of our family, not just in-laws.

The next day we were off to Normandale Lutheran Church in Edina for the ceremony. Things went off without a hitch. There was almost a problem, though but averted because I am unable to throw much away. One of my son's fraternity brothers was going to read something written by Martin Luther King, Jr. and less than 5 minutes before the ceremony he said that he didn't have his copy. As the wedding coordinator began to go nuts, I recalled that what I think was the reading was on the back of a sheet of paper I was keeping notes on regarding the wedding . . . safely in my "bag of information mom dragged along to the church." The photographer ran to the room where we had changed and found my bag; I pulled out the paper, and the reading was retrieved.

By the way, the photographer, who had taken many family pictures over the years, came into the changing room just as we were finished dressing to take some candid photos of the bride and all as we prepared for the walk down the aisle. He was in a hurry, and I was all dressed except I had pulled my gown over my slacks and hadn't pulled them off yet. I was having trouble getting them down and over my shoes and without blinking an eye the photographer, Mr. Peterson, set down his camera, kneeled down and pulled off my slacks. Well, all the gals hooted and said he looked like he'd done that before. It released tension and was good for a laugh.

We offered to pay for the flowers, so Amy and I went to the "family" florist in a small strip mall in a neighborhood in Edina. It was a wonderful and fragrant afternoon as Amy made her selections. She went with vibrant and tropical colors and flowers that were fantastic. I was very pleased that she wanted to include some ivy in her bouquet that has some history. When Joon and I were married 30 years before Erick and Amy's wedding, there was ivy in my bouquet from our Church ceremony. We returned to Korea after our wedding in Willmar, MN, but my mom rooted the ivy and potted it for me and tended to it until we returned over a year later. All those years (and still today) I kept at least two plants growing from that original ivy. So we asked the florist if he could put some in Amy's bouquet which he was glad to do, just asked that I bring it in the day before the wedding. Well, I just grabbed one of the plants when I went to the beauty shop (in the same strip mall) the day before the wedding and he used it in her bouquet. I still have 3 plants growing, and if our daughter marries we hope she will want to carry on the tradition.

After the pastor welcomed everyone to the wedding, my husband got up and did the same in Korean. A great number of out-of-town guests were from Korea or were Korean-Americans from New York, L.A., etc, so he wanted them to feel comfortable and welcome. We had lots of ladies in silk Korean traditional dresses, and the wife of our friend from Japan wore her kimono. There were so many people from so many cultures that it was a real internationally festive atmosphere.

For the lighting of the Unity Candle, we lined up on both sides of the couple facing the guests . . . first the bride or groom, then their parents, then their grandparent, and the candle started with the grandmothers on the far out sides, then to the parents, then to the bride and groom who joined the two candles to one. During this time, our daughter Sonja played a magnificent flute solo, and we received so many compliments from guests that felt it was so personal as we all stood there and actually commented back and forth, smiled to the guests and kind of got everybody into the emotion of the moment.

The stretch limo that we hired to take the wedding party from the church to the park for pictures, then to reception was great, except for one little thing. On the hottest day in June, the air conditioning broke down and they sweltered in their tuxedos and long dresses and didn't enjoy the heat much at all. Guess you can't get hitched without a hitch.

The reception venue was all up to the bride's parents, but we got to go along to the tasting with her parents and the bride and groom to decide on the menu. It was at the old grand train station in downtown St. Paul, with the Greek columns out front and just as beautiful inside. Each table had its own cake, and those at the table cut and served it whenever they felt like it. I've been at many weddings where it seemed they never got to serving the cake until many people had already left. The individual cakes was an idea they had learned about at a friend's wedding, and since their wedding I have seen it done at other weddings too. But there was no cake top to save for the first anniversary. So, for their first anniversary, I decorated a small two-tiered traditonal-style wedding cake and surprised them with it.

We ate and danced and had a wonderful evening. Erick gave a speech to everyone that was so moving. It was truly the happiest day of his life.

We gave them a honeymoon in Hawaii for a gift. They were in Maui in a condo on the ocean for 10 days and had a wonderful time. We received a note on a postcard from the honeymooners:

"Dear Mr. & Mrs. Chi & Sonja

Its us, Mr. and Mrs. Chi from Maui. What can we say about Maui? The scenery/weather is incredible. So far we have spent most of our time lounging around and laying about on Maui's pristine beaches, breaking occasionally to imbibe some of the delicious salt water fare the Pacific Ocean is so famous for.

I'm finding that as a husband I have to keep on my toes. The last time I fell asleep next to the pool, I awoke to the melodic advances of a smooth talking flemish octogenarian trying to seduce my wife under the guise of "borrowing suntan lotion." Don't worry, I put a stop to that quite promptly. Anyway we have a lot more yet to do, including continuing to gorge ourselves on fish, shrimp and other creatures of the briny deep. Love you!

Amy & Erick"

We got a post card from them a year later when they went to Mexico on vacation that read:

"Mom and Dad,

Camp is fun. The counselors keep making these things called pina coladas that Amy seems to be drinking a lot of. But that's ok. We have to be careful not to drink the water or we'll become too 'regular.' The hotel is beautiful, the weather is warm, and the locals like to stare at my wife. Aside from that last part, this is a pretty darn good trip. Hope you're not too jealous, Erick." Added at the bottom was a note from Amy that read *"Dear Mom and Dad, We're going to take a day trip to the Mayan ruins tomorrow. I'm very excited about that. Camp's been fun but there is this Erick boy that won't leave me alone . . . Love you, Amy"*

Now that I include these in my book, I'm wondering if Erick or Amy wouldn't be better at writing this . . . they do have a way with words. Erick's college entry essay for George Washington University, which was done in the wee hours of the night at the very last minute, was fantastic. Anything he wrote came alive on paper. I always wished I had saved more of his papers from school over the years. Amy's essay for medical school was also so creative and well written. If I had a copy I would have included it in this book.

As I write this chapter, Erick and Amy have had a few more anniversaries and also now have a toddler cutie named Annie and a second baby on the way. She was born about 9 months after their 1st vacation to Mexico. She gave "made in Mexico" a whole new meaning. It is unbelievable the effect grandchildren have on us. She is so special words cannot describe it. Now I realize why my parents were so thrilled when we had our kids.

Chapter 9

Don't Bury Someone in a Rented Tuxedo

(My Dad, the Church, My Faith)

When my father passed away, we considered burying him in the tuxedo he always wore when performing with the Nordkap Men's Chorus, a Norwegian men's chorus that he belonged to for many of his later years. However, at the last moment my mom decided on a different set of clothes, and we scratched the tuxedo idea. The Nordkap Men's Chorus sang at dad's funeral wearing the very tuxedo that we had considered. A couple of weeks after the funeral a member of the chorus called my mom and stopped by her house to pick up the tuxedo. Unknown to us, the tuxedo did not belong to dad but was owned by the chorus.

Even in the midst of grief, there is often humor. It is just difficult to see through the tears and allow the laughter to break through. Our son Jon died when he was 6 $\frac{1}{2}$ years old. Our daughter was born about 2 years later. She was known in our church for being a bit noisy during the service. During one service when she was in her terrible 2's she was behaving rather badly. During this same service, the pastor was handing out first Bibles to the 3rd graders—the group that should have included our son Jon. I couldn't help the tears during this time. A lady behind us in church tapped me on the shoulder and said, "Don't worry about her bad behavior. It happens to children all the time and we understand." Little did she know that my tears had nothing to do with Sonja's behavior!

After years of being a little demon during church, our daughter Sonja was assigned the role of an Angel in the Christmas Pageant—back when there used to be Sunday School Christmas Pageants with costumes, memorized lines and wonderful memories. Well, I volunteered to make the wings and halos for all of the Angels. I bent and re-bent wire coat hangars until they formed beautiful wings. I sprayed them with glue, covered them with gold glitter, used some gold festooning (garlands) and when put on over the white children's choir robes, the group of girls was transformed into the most beautiful angels I had envisioned. However, the evening did not go without incident. Prior to the beginning of the program, the Youth Director fell and was taken away by ambulance with a seriously broken ankle. And, when the Angels marched in and went "on stage", Sonja's wings caught in the decorations of the 20-foot Christmas tree, and the audience gasped as the tree began to topple towards her until an usher grabbed it and averted a near catastrophe.

About 2 weeks after our son Jon died, our son Erick, who was then 3 years old, sang a solo at the Sunday School Christmas Program at the Church where the funeral had been held. He had a great voice, even at such a young age, and I had taught him a Christmas Carol in Norwegian, "Jeg Er Sa Glad" which means I Am So Glad [on Christmas Eve]. He sang it without any piano or organ accompaniment, just his Sunday School teacher holding a mike in front of him. In the darkness and quietness of the evening, and the flickering of the candles, it was a breathtaking moment, and I don't think there were very many dry eyes in the church that night. I don't recall Erick ever singing another solo in church or school for many, many years. He told me he didn't want to be the center of attention, just in the back row was fine for him. A year or two later, he was cast as the hump of a two-humped camel, a role which he probably just loved . . . . don't recall if he was the front hump or the back hump.

Sonja took to the stage a lot in middle school and in high school. She loved the theatre and was active on stage and behind the scenes. In one middle school production, she and another actor, who were not in the current scene, chose to sit down on the bed that was behind a curtain and only opened during other scenes. Well, she and the young boy who sat down on the bed were more than startled when someone opened the wrong curtain, and there the two sat, on the edge of the bed, swinging their feet, passing the time. They scurried off the stage like two bolts of lightening, and the audience enjoyed the comic relief provided during a rather serious production.

When my great aunt Olga passed away, her grave was dug in a cemetery holding many of my ancestors in Cyrus, Minnesota. However, after the service, when the funeral procession made it's way from Morris to Cyrus, little did we know that during the night a skunk had accidentally fallen in the hole and in the frantic scurrying that must have occurred when it realized it was trapped, had sprayed only the odor that a skunk can release. Were the tears at the funeral for the passing of Aunt Olga, the sting of the odor, or a bit of both?

When my cousin Dennis died, his funeral was in a suburb north of Minneapolis and at least 30 miles from the National Cemetery at Fort Snelling where he was to be buried. My daughter went along with me to the funeral and offered to do the driving. When we left the funeral home, we were about the 5th car behind the hearse and little did we know that the drive to the cemetery would be one of the most stressful drives. First, the hired motorcycle cop drove up and down the fleet of cars, yelling at us to turn on our lights . . . not in a nice way either, but in a demanding and scary voice. Then the entourage pulled out onto the main highway, and the fun began. We were supposed to keep together. The cops were to cut off other cars at intersections and wave us through red lights, etc. All went fine until we pulled onto the main freeway. With all of the lanes and traffic, it was impossible to keep the string of 15-20 cars together. Well, we lost track of the car in front of us and discussed the best way to get to the cemetery without them. However, we realized that everyone behind us still thought we were in the funeral procession as we took an exit, and they, of course, all followed us. We ended up arriving at the cemetery before the hearse and the first 5-6 cars behind it, so we waited within the cemetery until they arrived, then followed them over to the burial site. Sonja mentioned something about NEVER going with me to another funeral or something to that effect!!

In the small town Norwegian Lutheran Church, St. Petri, where I grew up, there are lots of memories. The congregation was small, and we had "our pew" which is where we sat each Sunday. Nobody ever sat in someone else's pew. This brings back the old joke about not farting in church because you have to sit in your own "pew". I digress. One Sunday, during the sermon, a candle on the altar dripped onto the cloth and began to flame up. As the pastor continued, a farmer seated near the front of the church got up, jumped over the altar rail, pulled off his shoe, and stomped the fire out with it. The pastor bowed his head and waited for Stanley to finish. When the fire was out he turned around, went back over the altar rail instead of walking around, and back to his pew, and the pastor continued. Maybe Stanley was too used to going over the fence to get the cows! After church the pastor told my father that he wanted to say something about his sermon being so hot that it started the fire but thought better of it.

We had an old Dr. in our town called Doc Linde. He was quite interesting. We never went to him as a family doctor, but he would come to the school to check heights and weights and tonsils. One year he looked down my throat and said that my tonsils looked good. I had had them removed several years earlier by our family doctor. He also gave physicals that were required by Bible Camps in those days. Well, he checked my eyes, ears, throat, listened to my heart, and called me fit to go to Camp. However, my two girlfriends who were cute, curvy and cheerleaders at the school also went for their physicals, and he had them strip to the waist. Me, my physical was fully clothed!!

This same old Doc Linde had delivered my father at their home above the Cyrus Leader newspaper office in 1918. He said "Oh, this baby weighs about 13 lbs." and that is the only official information regarding dad's birth other than the date and location.

Doc Linde also thought he could play the violin. One New Year's Eve he was on the program for the annual New Year's

Eve Service. He had a pretty young high school girl, nicknamed Swen, accompany him on the piano. The program was in the sanctuary of the church. Well, he sawed away at the violin for awhile and finally said, "Well, that's enough of this damn thing!" and sat down. My friend Jimmy turned purple he laughed so hard, as did we all!!

In college I played the trumpet. Our concert band went on tour each winter and one year went to the Pacific Northwest, one year to Chicago and another year we toured the upper Midwest. Well, upon returning from one of these tours, we talked the bus driver into having a Chinese Fire Drill on the bus at an intersection a few blocks from our destination, our return to Augsburg College. For those of you who don't know about a Chinese Fire Drill it was usually done with a car at a red light, and the driver would call it, everyone would exit the car, run around it, and get back in before the light turns green. The whole bus load would be a challenge, but we wanted to give it a try. When the light turned red and the bus stopped, we bailed out of the door and had not factored in the ice. Well, to make a long story short, Ed, who played bass horn in the band and cello in the Augsburg Orchestra, hit the ice, took a header and fractured his arm or wrist, and we spent several hours across the street in the emergency room getting him "cast".

My sister Karen has been plagued her whole life with feet that not only hurt, but are a bit deformed from birth. In fact, when she was born, her legs were somewhat twisted and blue and the doctor told my parents that she may never walk. Well, they straightened out, but she has suffered with leg and feet problems her whole life. But, she never loses her sense of humor. Buying shoes is always torture . . . nothing fits well, nothing feels great and of course nothing looks pretty. She told her husband some years ago to bury her in 3" stilettos as finally her feet won't hurt, but they'll look great! She also insists that lunch be served after her funeral because she has been in food service her entire life and has done lots of catering for weddings and special events and she finally wants someone else to prepare the food and serve it.

After my mom spent a few years in an assisted living facility which cost her about $3500 a month, the money began to run out. Eventually she had to go to a nursing home where she would get more care. Of course, that was even more expensive. I did the paperwork necessary to obtain assistance from Hennepin County for her care. In order to qualify, you must be just about out of money completely, which she was. However, one thing they encourage you to do is to go to a funeral home and purchase a pre-paid funeral. This makes good sense, and I contacted Morris-Nilsen Funeral Home (MN) in Richfield and prepaid $7500 initially plus $2000 more later on just before mom's money was totally gone. This money is invested by MN and interest earned is added to the principle, so it is hoped that as costs of funerals rise so will the value of the pre-paid amount. This pre-paid funeral includes all funeral home costs and can be used for flowers, a meal following the service, cemetery markers—literally any expense directly related to the funeral. Well, in 2008 her pre-paid funeral funds earned over $600 in interest. Well, I wish our 401K or investments would have gained, but we lost in the market big time!

Mom's need for nursing home care was first due to short term memory loss and has continued to worsen along with generally deteriorating health. She is 89 years old. On one recent visit, when she was having trouble completing a thought, she exclaimed, "You might as well put me in the Home, I can't remember a thing." She still thinks she is in her assisted living apartment I think. It is sad, but some comments are truly funny.

At a recent pot luck with several of my cousins, we were sharing stories of our aging parents. One cousin, who is divorced, was caring for her father one afternoon a week while her sister took their mom for kidney dialysis. Her father suffered from dementia also. One afternoon while they were visiting he asked his daughter if she was married, not remembering she was his daughter. She said, "No, I'm divorced," to which he replied sadly, "Oh, we have that in our family too!"

My cousin Bruce, whose mom is a dedicated MN Twins baseball fan, says that he knows how to keep her happy when she is old and forgetful. He says he'll just tape a great Twins game that they win and just play it over and over for her 'cause it will be new each time.

Dementia is very sad, and because it is so hard to see, we often joke about it in order to deal with it at all. Will I get old enough and forgetful enough that I can hide my own Easter eggs? Maybe so. I think the most difficult time is when they go through a time when they don't even realize their memory is really poor. I witnessed several things with mom that were very disconcerting for me. Once I was with her when she was asked for ID at Lund's grocery store, something they routinely did, and she complained to the clerk that in all the years she had shopped there, they had NEVER asked her for her ID. We would go to restaurants, and she would think it was the first time she had been there, yet it had been places we had gone with her many times before. Those things are hard to watch. Then she got to the point where she realized her memory wasn't good, and it frustrated her. She "covered" and often said, "Oh yes, I remember now" or something similar when we knew she was covering. For mom, it seems that now that she only really has memories of the "olden days" she seems less agitated and comfortable. She still remembers stories of when she was a kid, remembers the words of lots of old hymns and and songs. The care givers at the nursing home say that she has mostly talked of growing up on the farm and "the boys" meaning her brothers. Recently, her brother Mervin played a tape of songs that he had of their mother singing children's songs and mom sang along with almost every one and enjoyed it. Yet, she doesn't know what she had for dinner only a few minutes after the meal and thinks all of her clothes are new because she doesn't remember ever wearing them. For a long time she participated in weekly sessions of "Name That Tune" at the nursing home. Often she would be able to name a song in 2-3 notes . . . they played old songs, and she almost always was the first to name the tune.

The visits to see mom get tougher and tougher. Many times the ride home is long and lonely. A few times when I've gone to visit her, I've not gotten in to do so. I drive the 35 miles and find no place within my walking distance to park. As I lose weight I've found I can hobble a little further, but I cannot go a block or more. So sometimes I've waited 45 minutes with no parking opening up and finally, gone back home and planned to go again soon.

She's no longer the mom I knew. She wasn't a perfect mom, but I loved her, and she was a lot of fun. My dad went through the same memory loss thing 10 years ago and passed away at 80 years of age. However, added to his mental state was a lot of paranoia and some rather bizarre thoughts of what was going on around him. That was even tougher. Towards the end, neither of them remembered us which is the hardest of all. I just focus on the wonderful memories of having both of my parents until they were in their 80's. Mom will be 90 on her next birthday. And although she won't remember the party the day afterwards, we'll still celebrate because no matter what, she enjoys the moments when she is with family and friends.

Author's note: Mom passed away after this manuscript had been submitted to the proofreader. I have added the following thoughts I had after the funeral was over. Some thoughts have already appeared in the book, but I left this intact for continuity.

*   *   *Tribute to Mom*   *   *

When my father passed away in 1998, mom was already showing signs of memory loss. It was subtle, and her ability to cover for her forgetfulness was very good. I look back now, after she is gone, and think how she must have suffered emotionally. I don't know if she ever discussed it with anyone but she never shared her feelings about it with me. She knew she forgot things. I think she knew she was covering. When she finally began to acknowledge her memory problems, she would talk about it a bit but we didn't dwell on it. She asked me once, several years ago, if she was doing anything strange or weird. I told her that her memory was obviously a problem, but she wasn't doing anything strange or embarrassing. I told her, "Mom, if you start to wear your pants outside of your dress, I'll tell you!" She laughed and we laughed. She seemed to be more comfortable with her memory problems when she

I assured her that she wasn't doing anything embarrassing. As dementia worsens I often wonder at what point the recipient of this horrible disease gets past knowing that they are losing their memory. Now when I don't remember something it bothers me. However, when my family or friends remind me of something I usually remember it and don't very often draw a total blank. I worry about ending up like mom. When you have been so close to someone with memory problems it is difficult not to be concerned that the same thing may happen to you. I am constantly trying to learn or do something new (crafts, reading, board games, computer games, writing, swimming, researching subjects, etc.) to use different parts of my brain and keep it stimulated. I multi-task well . . . so far. I hope to keep it that way.

After mom had been in the nursing home for a few months she was openly having memory problems. She said, "I have such trouble remembering things, you might as well put me in the home." A few years ago, that would have been funny. And mom had a fantastic sense of humor. But this time the comment was not funny. She still thought she was in her assisted living apartment.

As mom's memory loss worsened and worsened the long term memory seemed to remain intact. She spoke more and more of the 'olden days' and the good part about this was that the many stories were fun to listen to. The staff at the nursing home said that she shared so many memories of "the boys," which means her four brothers; and growing up on their farm in Northern Minnesota. Most of the staff at the nursing home knew a lot about her life growing up, and knew almost nothing about her husband or her children. Her most vivid memories were of her childhood. The last few months I would show her pictures of dad or my sisters, or my children, and she wouldn't know who they were. We brought two pictures to her room of her first great grandchild and she just called the pictures "the twins". You have to see the humor in that or dealing with someone with dementia would be impossible.

Before mom was homebound I used to pick her up and go for drives. She loved to go to the Dairy Queen and used to go with my sister Kathy on many trips to DQ too. As we drove down familiar streets she would comment on buildings, businesses, etc. and comment over and over about how many new things there were. In fact, almost nothing was new. It was the same route we always took, but her short term memory loss caused her to forget.

While she was in assisted living she always knew her way to the dining room or mail pickup and never got lost returning to her mini-apartment. Mom never wandered off or away from her room and dining room in the nursing home either. This was partially due to the fact that she had become so frail that she no longer used her walker. She was confined to a wheelchair. She used her feet to help move her wheelchair and would leave her room but never went beyond the elevator lobby area which was across from her room; and the dining room which was just beyond the elevators. She never showed any interest in getting on the elevator or even to go out of her room and turn to the left instead of the right. This wandering can be a problem with patients with memory loss—at least there was one thing we did not have to be concerned about. Because she was not at risk for getting on the elevator or trying to go out of the building or off her 5th floor unit, she was not moved to the floor designated for memory loss residents. I was glad I didn't have to observe that floor.

When mom was still driving I would make sure to always drive the same route to church or to the store with mom to imprint the directions in her memory. Giving up driving was pleasantly simple. She easily gave up driving. Part of her problem was that she used a walker and the distance in her condo from the elevator to the parking spot for her car was too far for her to walk, and she was not able to put the walker in and out of the car by herself. When I took her for rides, I made her put her walker in and out of the car herself as long as she could, but it wasn't long until she was unable to do so.

Mom lived in a luxury condo, Point of France, when dad died in 1998. She got along very well for the first year or two. Soon her walking was a problem. She fell a couple of times and wasn't able to get up. One time she fell and slid on her butt down the hall, which was 20' long, before she got to a phone to call for help. She was black and blue from the fall, but luckily nothing was broken.

My sisters and I decided to talk with mom about her moving to an assisted living facility. We convinced her that it would be good for her to make the move while she was able to make the decision instead of waiting until we had to make the decision for her. I took her to visit several assisted living facilities and she liked the one in Bloomington called Meadow Woods. Meadow Woods was a wonderful facility. It was not too huge and had a very nice atmosphere. The dining room was lovely and they used stemware and cloth napkins. It seemed like a nice restaurant, not an institutional dining room.

We had some good family times while mom was at Meadow Woods. They had private dining areas directly off the regular dining room and we had some birthday celebrations there with mom, our kids, my sisters, her brothers who lived in Minnesota, and sometimes a niece or nephew or two of mom's. A couple of times I went over there on Sunday morning and attended church with mom at the little chapel. Most of the time she watched their service on closed circuit TV in her room. At Christmastime they usually had a service for families to attend. One year my sister Kathy and my daughter Sonja and I went over to attend the Christmas candlelight service with mom. There was a bell choir from a local church playing carols. It was a beautiful service. It was held in the dining room and we sat at the tables during the service. The bell choir was seated in chairs in a "U" shape and our table happened to be behind the "U" so we were right behind some of the bell ringers. The bell ringers were all older ladies. They had been sitting quite awhile and when they were done playing they stood up to leave and the lady right in front of us passed gas much to our delight (and probably to her relief!). We four giggled like teenagers and laughed about it often. Even with poor memory, mom delighted in anything funny. Her mother always said "A good laugh is like a bowl of prunes." Mom carried on that saying.

For Thanksgiving or Christmas Day some of us would often join mom for dinner. On one occasion the administrator went from table to table serving wine. The food was wonderful and it was so nice to eat with mom. It was difficult to take mom out for meals, but she enjoyed having us join her as much as we enjoyed doing so. Times with mom, even until almost the end were always fun. She loved to laugh and so does her family. Until just four months before she died, we could joke and enjoy her company and we will try to remember those times and forget the slow ending.

Mom grew up in the depression and I think that is probably why she squirreled away all kinds of things from the dining room. While she was in assisted living I would go over once in awhile to get her laundry and do a little cleanup of her room. She had a bedroom, adjoining living room, bathroom, and large walk-in storage room. I would find coffee creamers, foil wrapped butter packs, cookies, cartons of milk, plates with cake, silverware, packets of crackers, etc., etc. They would be tucked away in drawers, behind the lamp, on the bookcase shelves and even under her recliner. Not being familiar with assisted living situations or nursing homes, this struck me as rather odd. My sister Karen and her husband have been managers of food service in nursing homes and similar facilities and they assure me that mom's hoarding was nothing compared to the pros they have witnessed.

The TV remote controls are a real problem when you begin to lose memory. Somehow she would get the one from her living room into the bedroom and vice versa and of course neither one would then work. We'd go over there, figure it out and it would be ok for awhile, but continued to happen.

Mom loved to watch Wheel of Fortune on TV and she and my sister Kathy watched it together via the telephone until mom moved to the nursing home. Something else mom loved was word games. She always had a pad and pencil handy. She would write a word or phrase at the top of the sheet of paper, then write as many words as she could using the letters from the core word or phrase. She was amazing at word games. When we were growing up mom played Canasta with us a lot. We played Scrabble. Every time we were in the car we would look for the alphabet, in order, on road signs; we'd count stuff; and we'd look for stuff while playing car bingo.

Mom loved music. We sang lots growing up and often in the car. Mom taught us lots of songs that her mother taught her years ago. She played the piano, but not from written music but from the heart. She never took lessons, but when she was younger she could pick up and play a lot of familiar tunes without any musical notes in front of her. She sang beautifully too. She was always on key and on the beat.

When mom moved into the nursing home I ordered her a telephone. She would try to change the TV with the cordless phone and dial the remote to make a phone call. I gave her a written list of our phone numbers, but it wasn't long until she couldn't figure out how to use the phone. I felt so bad when I ordered her phone service removed. It also meant that we could no longer pick up the phone and talk to mom. I missed that a lot and I know my sisters did also. I don't know if mom ever thought about not having a phone. She never asked where it was. Often when I would be with her in her room, and if she seemed to be doing pretty well, I would call one of my sisters (or sometimes both) and she would talk to them. A couple of times we called her brother Norris as he wanted so badly to talk to mom. That went on until the last few months when she could not put together phrases or sentences and conversing was no longer possible.

I had become her perfume supplier after dad died, and it got so that her room in the assisted living facility reeked Red Door, her clothes reeked Red Door and I started getting calls from the Administrator that her strong perfume was bothersome to staff as well as people who shared the table with her in the dining room. I knew we had a problem because I was buying Red Door every couple of months. I started diluting it with half water, but I think her sense of smell was getting worse because it disappeared twice as fast. Also, I think she simply forgot she had put on her perfume so did it again and again whenever she saw the bottle. When I brought home her clothes to do her laundry, I left the bag in the garage until I put it in the washer or the smell would permeate our house. Even after the clothes were washed and dried the Red Door lingered on. This was hard for me to handle too, because mom was always so concerned about her appearance, hair, etc. and I'm sure she would have felt terrible if she had known how offensive the perfume had become. I brought her a milder perfume implying that I couldn't find the Red Door brand at the store. Eventually I simply "forgot" to buy more perfume. When we moved mom out of her assisted living apartment into a nursing home they would not refund any of our security deposit because they said they shampooed the carpet and couldn't get the perfume odor out of it and had to replace it all. Who knew perfume could be such a problem.

Remembering to take her few medications was very troublesome for mom. For awhile I depended on her to remember to take her meds. I would write notes on the bottles as to when to take the medicine and how many, in larger letters than the little print from the pharmacy. Later, I prepared charts on my computer so she could initial when she took her pills and keep track that way. Nothing seemed to work. She would remember to take the pill and forget to check it off on the chart, or she would check it off on the chart and forget to take the pill. I did not often find that she took extra doses, but rather that she missed a lot of doses. I would count pills and find that she was starting to miss more and more doses. The medications were for osteoporosis, fluid retention, and minor ailments but still important. Finally I had to have the Meadow Woods staff administer her medications. They provide all services, but each service you add is an additional charge. They charged extra to bring food trays to people's rooms. The last few months she lived at Meadow Woods she asked more and more for her food to be brought to her room. She was weak and frail and even the short walk to the elevator and dining room got to be too much for her. Eventually she started falling and one night a staffer was walking down the hall and heard mom yelling. She had fallen down in her bedroom and had somehow managed to get halfway under the bed with a bookcase on the floor trapping her there. It was evident to the staff and to us that it was time for another move . . . the final move . . . to a nursing home. The first nursing home we found for mom just did not seem to be a good fit. We decided to move her to Walker and it seemed great right away. The caring staff at Walker Methodist Health Center took mom in their arms and treated her very well.

During mom's time at Walker, I received a few calls from staff or from her nurse/doctor with Ucare. Most were simply about progression of her dementia and then her congestive heart failure that had been going on for awhile. One day the nurse practitioner called and gave me the information that they felt mom was beginning to experience the end of her life and they suggested I get hospice care for mom. Thus began the beginning of the end. I met with the hospice team. Hospice was accomplished without having to move mom from her room at Walker. She had people attending to all of her needs as always, plus some music therapy in her room, hospice volunteers to just sit with her, chaplain visits, a nurse, a social worker . . . a lot of wonderful people gathered around to carry mom home.

It was difficult to talk with mom the last few months. I dug through my hymnbooks and found the old Worship and Praise Hymnal that had belonged to my mom's dad and then to her, and now belongs to me. I brought the book with me and sang and sang, every familiar hymn. Most of the time mom would hold my hand tightly so I couldn't free it to turn the pages. One Sunday morning about a week before she died, I was singing and she was listening and smiling with her eyes closed. A nurse even joined me for a chorus of "Just as I Am" that morning. I had sung several hymns and mom said "What happened?" She hadn't asked a question or said more than a word or two for a few weeks and they never made sense. I said, "You mean why are you here?" and she responded by waving her arm along the bed and wall, as if to say yes. I told her that she had been sick and was in the room so she could be taken care of. She closed her eyes and I resumed my singing. She broke in and said "Hurry". I asked her if she wanted me to hurry and finish singing or to sing faster. She said "Go". I asked her if she wanted to go. She didn't respond, so I asked if she wanted to go and be with dad. She turned and looked at me and said "Oh, is that how it is going to be?" She had not said a clear, understandable sentence for so long I was stunned. It sent shivers up my spine and I actually felt a bit faint. She knew. She was ok with it. The hospice people told me that often people will rally towards the end and do things not thought possible. With God, though, all things are possible. Her words that day and her smiles that day will forever live in my heart. She had also had smiles and some comprehensible words to my sister Karen and her husband the day before when they visited her after driving from their home south of Chicago to visit.

A week later mom had drifted in and out of consciousness and finally the next Sunday she was comatose when I went to see her. Monday my husband dropped me off at Walker while he went to a funeral in Edina, planning to come back to get me afterwards. When I walked into mom's room she was totally unresponsive. Her eyes were partially open, but she showed no response at all. This was the first time she did not squeeze my hand when I held her hand. Her breathing was labored and her color was not normal. She was very puffy around her eyes and was being given morphine quite often to keep her comfortable. I was shocked at her appearance and knew immediately that we were close to the end. Shortly after I arrived, Pastor Dixie, our visitation pastor from Normandale Church arrived. She is a wonderful person, a former nurse, and compassionate pastor. I had met her before at mom's, but when she came in this time, she knew too that mom was in her last days. She read scripture (she said mom preferred the Psalms, which was not a surprise because she loves music and the Psalms are songs). She held a commendation service and when she finished and made the sign of the cross on mom's forehead after she and I had prayed over her. Mom stopped breathing for several seconds. Pastor Dixie and I looked at each other, both thinking that the end had come. But mom resumed her labored breathing. Pastor Dixie left. I sang only one more hymn because I could no longer get through a song without breaking down. I finally sat back in the chair and tried to rest. It was suddenly very lonely in that room.

When my husband called to say he was on his way I told him of mom's condition. He said that he would not pick me up, but park and come in and sit with me. He and I sat with mom for a couple of hours. Finally at almost 2:00 p.m. we decided to leave for an hour of so and get something to eat, and maybe even go home for awhile and come back later. I knew when we returned we would be staying until it was over. We both held mom's hands and told her we were leaving. I said, "Mom, it is ok to go. We'll all be fine." We walked out of her room, got on the elevator and got in our car. About 10-15 minutes later my cell phone rang and it was the nursing supervisor at Walker saying that mom had passed. Someone told her nurse we had left and about 5 minutes later she went in to check on mom and she had stopped breathing. It was simply over. We did not go back to the nursing home. We pulled over to the side of the road and began the barrage of calls that we would have to make. To call all of those people so close to mom who had been awaiting the call and dreading the call. To contact my sisters. To call my children. Our daughter and I had discussed what we should do if this happened while she was at work. She cannot receive personal calls at work and said that the only call I should make was if Grandma dies. She wanted to know right away. We called her at her office and told her that we were in the car and would drive to her office so she could get in the car with her dad and me and settle down before driving home. She took the rest of the day off. Other calls were made and Joon and I headed for home.

After years in assisted living at $3,500+ per month and then to a nursing home, mom's money eventually ran out. In order to get County Assistance for mom, I had to spend down all of her assets. We had sold her condo when she moved into assisted living so we had that equity to pay monthly expenses for a few years. The last item that had to be taken care of was to pre-pay mom's funeral in a trust with the funeral home of our choice. I did that, notified the county that mom's assets now were under $2,000 and suddenly the paperwork and hassles decreased noticeably. It was simple. I had to provide the County with an annual update on mom's financial situation. Other than that, I had to send almost her entire Social Security check to the County and in turn they covered all of her nursing home care costs. I was allowed to keep a small amount of money in her checking account and that was enough to buy her clothes, pay her beauty shop bill and pay other incidentals that were very minor. Maybe there is only one good thing about mom's memory loss. She was never aware that she was being supported by County funds. It isn't something she would have ever imagined or felt comfortable about. But its the reality. There was no choice. We are thankful to be in a country where mom would still receive quality care, even as her circumstances changed.

To say the least, the mountains of paperwork involved in being Power of Attorney for aging parents is unbelievable. The responsibility is awesome. I was lucky in that my two sisters were supportive and did not disagree with issues. I included them in all major decisions regarding dad, and later mom. However, I held the Power of Attorney so was ultimately responsible for the decisions that were made and that they be carried out. I can't imagine how it would have been if decisions about our parents were cause for infighting as does happen in some families. We have our issues, but not as they related to the care of our parents. That is a great thing!

Here is the story about mom that was on the back of the church bulletin at her funeral:

Vivian Dorothy Felt *was born June 9, 1919 near Bagley, Minnesota, to Axel and Nora Felt. After Vivian, the Felt's had four more children—Lloyd, Norris, Mervin and Orville. They lived on a small farm near Itasca State Park. She graduated from Bagley High School.*

Ernie Tinseth was a young student at Augsburg College when he was asked to go to Bagley to teach summer Bible School and assist the pastor of a 5-church parish during the summer vacation. One of those 5 churches was Sell Lake, a small country church near Itasca State Park. Vivian was playing the organ at Sell Lake Church when Ernie first saw her. He always said it was truly "love at first sight." They were married in 1941 and they resided in Cyrus, Willmar, and finally Edina. Vivian was a member of Federated Women's Clubs and held offices at the Local, State and National level. That participation included the opportunity to have lunch at the White House during a trip to Washington, D.C. many years ago.

While a member of St. Petri Church in Cyrus she was Sunday School Superintendent and taught Sunday School. She was always involved in Ladies Aid and Bible Study Groups. She continued to be an active church member at Calvary Lutheran Church when she and Ernie moved to Willmar in 1964, and Oak

Grove Lutheran Church when they moved to Edina in 1985. After Ernest passed away in 1998 she joined Normandale Lutheran Church in Edina.

Vivian's short term memory began to fail her many years ago, but until just a few months ago she charmed everyone at the nursing home with stories about the "boys" (her 4 brothers), and growing up on the farm. Staff at the nursing home said she told story after story of the fun they had growing up and the great times she had with Ernie and their daughters and later her grandchildren. She bragged with the best of them. And, on Tuesday night's "Name that Tune" at Walker she was tough to beat. If there was an old song, she knew it—often with just 3 notes!! This past Christmas she didn't remember names when family came to visit, but when Carolers stepped off the elevator to sing she sang every word with them. She always kept her sense of humor and one day a few months ago said that we might as well put her in the home 'cause she couldn't remember anything!

She lived in Meadow Woods Assisted Living in Bloomington for a couple of years before moving to Walker Methodist Health Center in March of 2007.

Vivian is survived by four brothers; daughters Karen Nord (Mike) of Plainfield, IL, Phyllis Chi (Joon) of Shakopee, MN, and Kathleen Jackson (Bruce) of Edina; grandson Erick Chi (wife Amy) and their daughter Annie; and grand daughter Sonja Chi. She was preceded in death by husband Ernest Herbert (1998) and grandson JonNamsun Tinseth Chi (1982).

And, here is a tribute I wrote that was an insert in the bulletin at her funeral:

Mom loved God

Mom loved Dad

And Mom loved us, all of us.

She taught us how to keep a house. When entertaining, the cleanliness of the house was more important than the food. My daughter says some things skip a generation and housekeeping may be my circumstance with that. Mom taught us to pick up after ourselves. The "10-minute pick-up" was the last swing around the house before going to bed at night so we would get up to a clean house in the morning. To this day, I often think about making a little swing around the house to put things in order for morning. Sometimes I even do it!

Mom wasn't a fantastic cook, but she WAS a fantastic baker. She made the best rosettes and donuts and cookies and deserts in town (no matter what town she lived in!!). She always had tins of great cookies in the deep freeze for unexpected company, especially at Christmastime. There were also gallon glass jars of donuts in the freezer. I think my sisters and I ate more frozen cookies on the sly than cookies served by mom. It is amazing how we could sneak into the basement and slowly open the deep freeze door to keep it from squeaking and enjoy cookies without mom knowing. At least we thought she didn't know.

Mom loved music. We sang in the church choir whether we wanted to or not. We took piano lessons whether we wanted to or not. We ended up all the better for it and all love music because of her. She even influenced dad with her love of music. He took piano lessons when we were kids, and in later years he joined the Nordkap men's Chorus. He liked music, but I think mom supported him so he got involved with it. She sang to us, we sang together, we sang in the car, and we always enjoyed good music (and even some bad stuff!). She taught Sunday School. Every fall I would wonder who my teacher would be and sure enough, it would be mom. She seemed to follow my grade each year. She didn't do this for all of us. I wonder if she thought I needed a bit more supervision than the other girls?

When I married a bit out of the traditional Norwegian-Lutheran tradition, she was so supportive and wonderful. She loved my husband as if he were her son. When our son was born with health problems, mom was always there for us . . . to support, to pray, to help in any way she could. She taught me *that your responsibilities as a mother never end. She was always so proud of her daughters and her grandchildren. She bragged with the best of them. She dearly loved her grandchildren. I wish she would have been able to enjoy her great granddaughter, but unfortunately she wasn't able to do so.*

She was always ready with advise. My children will probably attest to the fact that that did not skip a generation!! She often came back with a negative response to an idea, dad usually had the positive response to most ideas and between the two there was a real balance in our lives. We were blessed to grow up in a home full of faith and laughter and fun!

She taught us that women could be assertive and successful. Although she never attended college, I think most people would have never guessed she had not. It didn't matter. She was well read and very in tune with the world. She gave speeches in churches, at Women's conventions and led Bible Studies and was a teacher in so many ways. From Sunday School Superintendent to President of the Ladies Aide, she was often in a position of responsibility and authority. She was a take charge kind of person. She was very well educated . . . but she didn't need a degree to prove it.

She will be missed, but never forgotten.

She will be gone, but not from our hearts.

Bye mom, we all love you!!

In 1998 when my dad passed away, we wrote this story for the funeral bulletin:

Ernest H. Tinseth
May 1, 1918-May 29, 1998

Ernest Herbert Tinseth (Ernie) was born in Cyrus, Minnesota on May 1, 1918 to Anton and Severina. He was the big brother to three sisters, Ruby (Wolters), Doris (Johnson) and Lorraine (Eken). He was baptized and confirmed at St. Petri Church in Cyrus, graduated from Cyrus High School and attended Augsburg College and Seminary in Minneapolis. As a student at Augsburg, he was sent to Bagley, Minnesota to teach summer Bible School and assist the pastor of a 5-church parish during the summer vacation. One of those 5 churches was Sell Lake, a small country church near Itasca Park. Vivian Felt was playing the organ at Sell Lake when Ernie first saw her. They were later married and had 56 wonderful years together.

While living in Cyrus, Ernie farmed, owned the local gas station and Chevrolet dealership as well as a Minneapolis Moline dealership. He was very active in the community and in St. Petri Church, serving as Mayor for many years, and serving on the Church Council in many capacities. In the 70's they moved to Willmar where he owned a realty company and commodity brokerage firm for several years. He began real estate appraising while in Willmar and continued to do appraisals after moving to Edina in the mid 80's. He retired on May 1, 1997.

In recent years, he was active in Kiwanis Golden K and the Nordkap Men's Chorus, serving as president for a period of time. He was on the Board of Directors at the Point of France Condominium where they lived and recently served as President of the Association. He was always a supporter of Augsburg College and Luther Seminary, and pleased that all of his children graduated from Augsburg. Ernie was always an involved and respected member of the communities in which he lived as well as a successful entrepreneur.

Hobbies were few, but he enjoyed collecting coins, pocket watches and miniature replicas of cars and farm machinery. He began his interest in coins with a penny collection he received from his father.

He was a loving father to three daughters, Karen (husband Mike) Nord of Naperville, Illinois; Phyllis (husband Joon) Chi of Edina and Kathleen of Edina. He was proud "gramps" to grandchildren Erick and Sonja Chi.

Ernie is survived by his wife, sisters, daughters and grandchildren. He was preceded in death by one grandson, Jon Chi.

When my dad was going to nursing home care in 1998, he asked me to take over all of their finances and handle everything for them. I said I would try and do as good as he had, and he said, "Oh, I hope you can do better than THAT!" From that day forward, I did everything for both mom and dad with full Power of Attorney for both. The responsibility is tremendous and the paperwork and dealing with eventually selling their condo, and moving mom and keeping up on insurance, taxes, doctor and dental appointments, paying of bills, renewing prescriptions, etc. is quite overwhelming. I was still working the first 8 years of POA for them and still had kids in high school and college. I know when I retired, it was a relief for me to finally have some time for me. Since I retired I have been able to pursue some of my favorite hobbies and pastimes and am grateful for that. I have been fortunate to have the support of my two sisters, although they cannot share the day to day work, they appreciate and support me. and when I go to them for comments or input on decisions, they are very helpful. I have no idea how people get along that don't have a trusted family member to take over their finances. The very wealthy just hire attorneys, but for the working middle class, we have to fend for ourselves. Now that I've learned all of the ins and outs about caring for elderly parents, it is just like having learned all the ins and outs of child rearing. We do it once, and by the time we figure it out and maybe get it right, its over!

I grew up in a home where humor was always lurking. We grew up and still revel in Ole and Lena jokes. Unfortunately, with our super sensitivity these days one hardly dares tell a good Ole and Lena joke unless you are certain nobody in the audience will be offended. Certainly I don't like cruel jokes, but I think people are waaaaaay too sensitive about seeing the humor in real life. I have to put a couple of jokes in this book, so here are some old favorites:

On elderly sex

On hearing that her elderly grandfather had just passed away, Katie went straight to her grandparents house to visit her 95 year old grandmother to comfort her. When she asked how her grandfather had died, her grandmother replied, "He had a heart attack while we were making love on Sunday morning." Horrified, Katie told her grandmother that two people nearly 100 years old having sex would surely be asking for trouble. "Oh no, my dear," replied granny. "Many years ago, realizing our advanced age, we figured out the best time to do it was when the church bells would start to ring. It was just the right rhythm. Nice and slow and even. Nothing too strenuous, simply in on the Ding and out on the Dong." She paused, wiped away a tear and then continued, "and if that darn ice cream truck hadn't come along, he would still be alive today!"

On keeping up with the times:

Ole, Sven and Lars were sitting naked in a sauna. Suddenly there was a beeping sound. Sven pressed his forearm, and the beep stopped. The other two looked at him questioningly. "Dat vas my new pager," he said. "I've got one of dem microchips under da skin of my arm."

A few seconds later a phone rang. Lars popped his hand open, lifted it to the side of his head and proceeded to talk into his palm while keeping one finger in his ear. When he finished he slapped his knee with his hand and explained, "Dat vas my new cell phone. Da microphone is on da microchip under the skin on da palm of my hand and da speaker is right here in dis finger!"

Now Ole was feeling a bit behind the times. He decided he had to do something just as impressive. He stepped out of the sauna and went to the bathroom. When he returned there was a rather long piece of toilet paper trailing from his butt. Sven and Lars raised their eyebrows and stared at him. Ole looked back and exclaimed, "Vell, vould you look at dat . . . . I'm getting a fax."

My dad was known for always telling a good joke. It was all in the delivery. Some can tell jokes, and some cannot. My dad and my uncle Orv were two of the best I know. It was even more fun when Erick and Sonja were old enough to join in and enjoy the humor too. I remember one time my parents "went on the road" with their Ole and Lena jokes. They actually went to Hinckley and performed at a local bank's Christmas party. Back then a Christmas party could actually be called a Christmas party. Anyway, they also did a Valentine's party for the Nordkap men's chorus that dad belonged to. The favorite thing they did had to do with a joke that dad never finished because every time he would start the joke mom would stop him as if the joke was inappropriate to tell. He never did finish it in the routine, but afterwards he'd finish the story for anyone who asked.

Mom and dad complimented one another in many ways. Although he was a very domineering man, he was compassionate, giving and fair. He didn't say no unless he meant it and so when he did that was the end of the discussion. He had a lot of respect for the clergy, having wanted to be a preacher but not realizing that dream as he was called home from college before he graduated to work on the farm. He kept friends with many pastors over the years . . . men he had met and became close to while they were all students at Augsburg. He actually met my mom when he was sent by Augsburg to preach at her little country church near Bagley, Minnesota, when their pastor went on vacation. He did a funeral and also ran the Bible School that summer. He always said that when he saw mom playing the organ he thought that pretty young thing was the woman for him. He made friends with her brother Lloyd, and they would go fishing and on outings, and dad always asked Lloyd if his sister Vivian might like to go along. Pretty soon Lloyd wasn't invited along, and the rest, as they say, is history.

Dad was raised in the Lutheran Free Church (LFC) which ceased to be in 1963 when it merged with the American Lutheran Church. The LFC was small, congregations mainly in the Midwest and the Pacific Northwest. Because it had only one college, Augsburg, and one seminary, it was a close knit family. Originally Augsburg included the seminary, but later they were separated. Our families all went along to conventions. Our Bible Camps were small and intimate, and we got to know kids from other church families very well and looked forward year after year to seeing them at camp. Then, when I went to Augsburg there were a lot of kids that I knew from Bible Camp and youth activities my whole life.

The merger presented serious concerns to me. I was a senior in high school, and it threatened my way of life. Besides, the preacher in the ALC church in our town (the town only had 2 churches—one LFC and one ALC) smoked which I was shocked at when I heard it. Ya, I was that sheltered and narrow. The only thing about me, by the way, that was actually narrow!!! Anyway, the LFC would be brought into the ALC and would forever lose its intimate status. The merger later resulted in a new hymnal that left out some favorite LFC hymns, changed a word or two or a few notes, just enough to irritate me. The old Concordia hymnal that I grew up with slowly disappeared from the racks of the churches. I doubt whether any churches have it in use today. Mine is on the piano, and I open it and enjoy it often.

To this day, we are still in touch with old LFCers. However, when my generation is gone, there won't be anyone left to remember. We still try to go to congregations where the LFC is quietly surviving. All of the pastor friend's of my father have passed on, but some of their kids (my age) still keep in touch. Our ties were as close as any family.

When we moved to Edina in the late 70's, the first church we joined was Lutheran Church of the Master. It was a beautiful round church on France Avenue across from Byerly's. It's congregation was very old, but the small atmosphere and cozy feeling led us there. However, the pastor was not very aggressive,nor was the congregation, and over the years it continued to shrink in size. When Erick was old enough to begin Confirmation, we went to the meeting and he was the only one in his class for Confirmation. They planned to combine his class with another small church elsewhere in Edina that would make it a class of three. We decided that as much as we liked the church, we wanted to be in a church where there would be opportunities for our kids to participate in activities with classmates from school. We visited a couple of churches. One small one just off France Avenue did not feel welcoming at all. The pastor at the time is now a Bishop in the church. Anyway, we ended up joining Normandale Lutheran Church.

Normandale was great for our kids. There are some things about Normandale that have bothered me over the years, but I think most of it has to do with being brought up in a small church within the informal Lutheran Free Church. My dad used to tell his pastor friends that it was good to bring more people "into the flock" but not to forget about taking care of the "sheep" you already have. This is one place where large churches fall short. They get so large that they become big business. They try to regulate too much. You no longer marry, get baptized or move your membership from one Lutheran church to another without formal classes, counseling or even testing. The ritual of placing monetary gifts in the collection plate on Sunday morning is slowly being replaced with automatic deductions from our bank accounts . . . something I doubt I will ever do.

Shortly before my nephew and his wife moved to Hawaii, I went to the Pastor's study to ask if he would baptize their little baby boy in a private baptism before they leave. They weren't members of Normandale, and they wouldn't be around to take the classes required by new parents before baptism, so he refused. Can you believe any pastor who would refuse to baptize a baby when requested? Not me!

Many years later my sister and her boyfriend went to the church to plan a wedding . . . they were in their 50's and wanted just a small family ceremony. She had been a member of Normandale for many years and also has been cantor often during the service and a loyal member of the choir for years. She volunteered in the church office for awhile but is limited because she suffers from MS. Anyway, she made an appointment to meet with the pastor and when they refused to go through the series of classes and tests required prior to marriage, the Normandale Church refused to marry them. Again, rules and regulations. Nobody is going to talk two 50+ year olds out of getting married, so what was the point of the tests and counseling. The answer was just "no." Nobody at church even contacted them to try and discuss it and work something out that would satisfy the church's demands and Kathy's needs. Kathy has not been back to Normandale since that day they refused to marry them. I went with Kathy and Bruce to the judge in the County Office Building, along with a friend of their's, for their wedding in August of 2008. It is very sad to me that someone brought up in the church wasn't able to be married there.

Confirmation was a wonderful experience for both of our kids but it had its problems too. Erick went camping once in his life . . . he and his dad did an overnight with the Scouts once in elementary school. Erick, like many of us, prefers a bed to sleeping on the ground and enjoys the outdoors but is not crazy about sleeping with bugs and critters. Well, at the end of Confirmation's last year the class would go on a camping trip. It is great for bonding and fun for many. Erick wanted to go but didn't want to camp. I spoke with the Pastor and asked why they couldn't go to a camp with cabins, so some could camp inside and others could choose to camp outdoors. I also mentioned to him that the handicapped boy in Erick's Confirmation class would be able to go along if they went to a more accessible place. None of that mattered. According to people I spoke with, parents of other Confirmands, the Pastor enjoyed camping, hiking and canoing and this was his preference. I guess it didn't matter what the kids wanted . . . he had started this tradition and was not interested in changing it. When I tried to get signatures on a petition regarding the trip one parent told me, regarding the pastor, that it was "his way or the highway" and a petition was pointless. I was not aware of that, so don't know if it is true. The lady was a prominent member of the congregation so I listened to her and decided not to stir up a hornet's nest. Erick did not go on the camping trip.

When Sonja got into Confirmation she also chose not to go camping, so missed out on the experience also. I had given up even talking to anyone about the trip. However, a new wrinkle came up when it was time to plan the Confirmation Service for Sonja's class. Normandale was undergoing a large expansion and renovation, so services were being held in the church basement. The church elders decided to have the Confirmation Service at the Catholic Church just down Hwy. 100 from Normandale. Didn't Luther leave the Catholic Church? Well, we were going back. No amount of discussion got anywhere; the decision was made. I felt that many would rather have the service in the church basement, even if it wasn't ideal, rather than being confirmed at the Catholic Church. I didn't want to drive down Hwy. 100 and point out OLG (Our Lady of Grace Catholic Church) as where my daughter was confirmed. A few of the parents agreed with me but were reluctant to push the issue. So, on October 31, Reformation Sunday, the Lutherans were confirmed within the walls of the Catholic Church. The Pastor said from the pulpit that, "Martin Luther would be proud of this day." In my wildest dreams I can't imagine why Luther would be proud of this day. He left the Catholic church for many good reasons. I figure he probably was spinning in his grave at the stupidity of it all.

Normandale has 4 pastors, plus visitation pastors and youth directors, choir masters and a great organist. With a couple of thousand members, maybe they need that many pastors. However, there were, for many years, two major problems. The church was getting too small and so was the parking lot. Rather than a practical solution which would be to expand from the 2 Sunday morning services to 3 or 4, we added onto the sanctuary at huge expense and also eventually added 50 parking spots at a huge cost per spot. Why in the world wouldn't a church first expand the number of services? This would divide the total number of attendees into 3 or 4 "congregations" thus alleviating the seating problems inside and the parking problems outside. Again, I do not understand how spending so much money was preferred over just increasing the number of services. It seems that money could have been spent on missions or helping the poor in the US. The Sunday School is also busting at the seams. I wonder if they'll break down and add additional Sunday School times on Sunday morning or add onto the Sunday School wing? What do you think?

Because of my diminished mobility, I have missed two Palm Sunday services over the years. You see, they have the congregation meet in the parking lot and then march in with palm leaves. That is great. What is not great is that they cordon off the handicapped parking area on the main level in order to make a safe gathering place. This leaves just 3-4 handicapped spots on the lower level to accommodate all handicapped people. I contacted the church office to ask if they could block off a different area, but no change was made. The two times I went back home were because there was no parking within the distance I am able to walk. On one of these Palm Sundays I went extra early in order to park and went in to sit in the sanctuary. A church secretary came in the sanctuary and told the hand full of us who were seated that we were to go out and march in with the rest of the congregation. I was so upset I almost left and went home. I just remained seated there and ignored her order.

We moved out of Edina, so we haven't been attending Normandale for awhile now, partly because we moved 25 miles away from there. At one time we used to give generously every Sunday to the church. We have cut back our giving enormously. I feel that NLC is not the best steward of my money. They have many wonderful ways they use our offerings, but I think some things are unnecessary and don't support them. We still give but to Walker Nursing Home, Augsburg College, In Touch Ministries, St. Francis Hospital and other charitable organizations that I feel will make good use of our money too. I don't think churches need a quarterly fancy booklet to give out church information; the monthly newsletter is sufficient. I don't think they need to continue paying so much in postage and printing when a huge percent of the congregation is probably on the Internet. There would be a huge savings to get into the Internet other than just a Web page. The Stewardship committee sent out corn seeds to all members last year to have us plant the seeds to see how they grow. It is a great object lesson in sowing and reaping. But in a city church there are large numbers of elderly who live in assisted living or apartments as well as young and old who live in condos and apartments where this is no place to plant corn. What do you suppose was spent in postage and product to send us all packs of corn seeds?

Maybe these issues with NLC are picky on my part, but they all add or deduct from the formal church experience. I have been thrilled to be a member but also disappointed at times. The music is fantastic, the choirs wonderful. We have been blessed with pastors who put together some really great sermons. It has been difficult for me to be part of such a large congregation. I grew up in a small, intimate congregation. Today churches are run like big business, partly out of necessity.

There are classes for everything except funerals I guess. You can get your toenails clipped, blood pressure taken or leave your toddlers for daycare/preschool. You have bible study on a golf course, in the early morning before going to work, or meet at a pub downtown Minneapolis. Wine and cheese are served at a church outing to a museum. There is no end to activities available. It is good to see the huge facilities being used more and more, not just focusing on the few hours of services on Sunday morning. It is a tough balance for churches to maintain—preaching God's Word and reaching out to the community and beyond. I have visited a church in Shakopee but haven't found a new church home as of yet. This goes back to taking care of the sheep you have, not just getting a bigger flock. A church needs to do both. It isn't easy.

My faith has always been strong. I grew up in a Christian home where parents led by example in all things. A promise was a promise; we never missed a school or church activity, and if we could stand up we could go to school. There were no wimps allowed. We were disciplined by being cared for and cared about.

I only recall one time in my life when I received a much-deserved slap on my face. My mom always had me set her hair (which meant in pincurls in those days) on Saturday mornings before I could go out and be with friends. We usually did this in the kitchen. One Saturday she sat at the vanity in her bedroom and was telling me how lucky I was to be able to do this for my mother. Well, I forgot we weren't in the kitchen, so as she went on and on I stuck out my tongue at her. She saw it all in the mirror. And as quickly as I realized we were in front of a mirror, she whipped around and gave me a good whop across the chops. As I said, it was well-deserved.

My parents did not use vulgar language, we never had liquor in the house and my parents didn't ever frequent a pool hall or club to my knowledge. I remember the first time I saw either of them drink wine was after I was out of college. Even our little Lutheran Free Church used plain old grape juice for communion. The first time I ever tasted wine was at communion in a church that didn't offer a choice between wine and grape juice. Liquor was never served in any of the homes of our friends or relatives either. Nobody said don't drink . . . nobody did. I recall a family reunion in Willmar with dad's sisters and their kids and his mother's side of the family. Some of the cousins brought a cooler of beer, and you'd think they'd broken some kind of major law. I remember they kinda snuck out in the back yard to drink the beer, knowing it wouldn't be a welcome addition to the pot luck! To this day I have to work at being open minded about drinking and realize that many people do so responsibly. It still is something I don't do, but I no longer condemn those who do.

Smoking was another story. Mom never smoked, but dad smoked cigars. They are pretty nasty, and in later years he reserved a good cigar for an outing to buy a car or when he and his partner Ken would sneak off without mom and enjoy a good cigar. Still, to this day, when I smell a cigar I like it just because it reminds me of dad I suppose. I'm just glad I didn't ever start smoking 'cause with the trouble I have controlling my eating, I can only imagine quitting smoking would be something I wouldn't be able to do. I am thankful for all of those who don't smoke and sympathize with those who do and want to quit. The rest of you are on your own!

When I was in college, I did a paper for Contemporary Theology Class. It is amazing to me that I feel very much the same about God now as I did then. Here is the paper, exactly as written in March of 1967, my senior year in college:

INTRODUCTION

I honestly did not know quite how to handle a paper such as this, nor did I really know where to begin or where to end. This paper was definitely beneficial to me in that it gave me a chance to put down on paper some of the ideas that I have.

My lack of theological background I am sure, shows up quickly in writing.

It will be especially interesting to go back and read through this in a few years. I wonder how different it will be from my ideas then.

MY FAITH

GOD is the creator of the world. He is a vastness. I visualize no form of Him, nor feel the need to do so. He is everywhere present and we feel this presence at all times. He is all-knowing. I feel that God knows everything we are doing or will do. However, I don't feel our life is pre-determined by Him. We are free to choose what we want to do, but God knows what we will choose before we do so. He doesn't force us or have us do things in a pre-determined manner. I don't feel we can sit back and expect, through faith, our lives to go on and our problems to be solved by Him with nothing on our part. Faith in God will not automatically put gas in my ford when the tank is empty, nor will it help me pass a test that I haven't studied for. These things are up to us—to strive to attain those goals that we feel are not contrary to the will of God.

With God we are never alone. When we get to the end of our rope, we need only remember that His is longer than ours. If we repent of our sins and confess to Him, he will forgive us of them. Also, He answers prayer. He doesn't always say yes, but he always answers. I remember a girlfriend who once said "Be careful what you ask for in prayer—you might get it!" This may be good advice. I think one important thing we should remember is to go to God with our joys as well as our sorrows and in good times as well as bad. And, as Pastor Youngdal would say, "When our troubles seem unsurmountable, rise above them on wings of prayer." It is through the grace of God that we receive the salvation of our souls.

JESUS CHRIST is the Son of God. He was given by God into the world to save the world. He took human form and qualities and lived on earth. He died for our sins. It would be interesting to know what would happen if Jesus were to walk on earth today as He once did.

Jesus has always been presented to me as a loving, tender, understanding Savior. It is through our acceptance of Him as our personal Savior that we become Christians.

One thing I find hard to understand is the idea, which is stated in the Apostle's Creed of the church, that when He died on the cross, He descended into Hell. Granted, He died a human being's death, but He wasn't a non-believer (in Himself?) therefore, I don't think he descended into Hell

Of the Trinity, Jesus is the easiest to understand or comprehend. He had a human form, whereas God and the Holy Spirit do not. He walked on earth and people talked with Him as they would a friend. This is the old idea that seeing is believing. When I was younger, I had no idea of God or the Holy Spirit as there were no pictures of them like of Jesus and Angels. Of course, when you are younger, faith is especially hard to understand—everything had to be proven in black and white. Unfortunately, for some, they never outgrow this!

HEAVEN and HELL are the places of eternity. As soon as a person dies, his soul enters Heaven or Hell. And, on the judgment day, God will have with Him in Heaven all the Christians and everyone else will go to Hell. There will be a new Heaven and I believe the description of it in Revelations is what it will be like. I think there will be 7 gates, etc. I believe we will have a different body, yet we will recognize one another. Everyone will understand everyone else also, as in the Bible when the people were filled with the Holy Spirit and could understand things said to them in foreign tongues. I don't believe there will be any more angels than those who have been with God since the beginning of time. Nor do I think people will wear white gowns and play harps all the time.

I don't have a definite idea as to where Heaven is, but I do believe it does [exist]. I suppose it is "out there" but this really doesn't present a question to me. I believe it exists and the where is not the important thing.

Hell, on the other hand, is not a desirable place! I remember a number of years ago when I thought Hell couldn't possibly be as terrible as everyone said. I guess then I was just trying to fool myself.

Heaven and Hell are very real to me. I have no doubts as to their existence now and throughout eternity. However, I believe that after judgment there will be a new Heaven and a new Earth.

SIN is any act or thought which is contrary to the will of God (sins of omission and commission). There are not degrees of sin. How can one be worse, when the breaking of one commandment breaks them all? There are some things I feel are not sinful, yet I wouldn't do them. I feel sins are black or white and not "gray" as many people wish.

Man was born in sin—all men are sinful and must repent their sins before they will receive forgiveness for them.

The continuing presence of the devil temps us at all times. There are so many things that are direct instruments of the devil which most people don't even think about. A classic example of this is the Ouija Board.

GRACE, God's Reward At Christ's Expense. This is what I learned about grace a long time ago in Bible School.

The fact that grace is given so freely makes it hard to comprehend. It is a means of salvation. We do nothing to get grace, it is freely given. We don't receive grace, we receive salvation. It is God's Grace, not ours, and our salvation.

SALVATION is an open door. It is a free gift to all who accept Jesus Christ as their personal Savior. Salvation is open to us because of Jesus Christ's dying on the cross.

Salvation is the saving of man from "sin, death and the power of the devil. By the grace of God, we can attain salvation—through repentance and faith in God.

THE MISSION OF THE CHURCH is to proclaim the Gospel. Its purpose is not to provide a social program for us, but to help us strengthen our faith. The mission of the Church should also be to make us fit into God's world, and not try to make God fit into ours—for example, jazz in the liturgy and other things that try to make it more convenient to be "religious" and not too demanding.

This was pretty interesting for me to read after all these years. I didn't have a lot of trouble with the contents of the paper, but the last sentence blew me away. I do have heartburn with that sentence. Otherwise, I'm amazed at how little change there is in my feelings about the subjects in the paper.

Although generally I'm not outspoken about my beliefs, I do not have trouble talking about them or sharing them when appropriate. I, like my parents, try to live by example too. The old, "a picture is worth a thousand words" quote is a good thing to keep in mind. Goals I have had as a teacher, as a manager, a friend, wife, and as a mom are to try and deal with people kindly, to help them if they ask (and sometimes if they don't) and to be patient when it is sometimes impossible. Only those of you who read this and know me will know if I meet those goals all the time; some of the time; once in awhile; or never. You vote.

I learned a bit about fireworks when I was a kid. Seemed like every 4th of July somebody lost a finger or an eye with a firecracker accident. I was always scared of firecrackers because of that and have never lit one in my whole life. The closest I got was lighting and enjoying sparklers as a kid and then with my kids. The toughest thing was to wait until dark. In Cyrus, dad was one of the business men in town and was the mayor for many years. One year he decided to fork out some dough and buy "real" fireworks and set them off in the city ball park. He and a couple of other businessmen loaded the fireworks in the back of his pickup truck and went into the outfield to set them off while the bleachers were full of townspeople waiting for the show. Well, one went off and up in the air just as it should. After that we all witnessed a fiery show in the outfield, and the fireworks were over. Somehow they had set off the rest of the fireworks all in one fireball that all occurred in the back of dad's pickup truck, sending the 3 men to scatter for shelter. The show was over, and you could hear the men laughing out in the darkness of the outfield. So much for a fireworks display in Cyrus. The bed of Dad's pickup truck was blackened from the fireworks, and it was a good story he shared for years.

Dad liked to do other things for people of our town. He arranged for a school bus several years in a row and sponsored trips to Fergus Falls for kids to see the circus. If they couldn't afford a ticket, he provided it.

We had a dinky (one train car) that ran from little town to little town. As more people got cars, it became less and less necessary until finally it was discontinued. On the last trip between Cyrus and Morris, dad handed out candy bars to everyone who rode the dinky. Rides that last day were free.

When he was mayor he was also the only "law" in town. Sometimes when a drunk got belligerent and picked a fight or beat his wife, dad would lock them up in an empty boxcar down at the railroad tracks and let them sleep it off. One man continually beat up his wife. She would come to our house in tears. Finally, dad gave her enough money so she and her kids could take the bus to Minneapolis to live with her sister and get away from the abusive relationship. She never returned to Cyrus. Her husband was never sober. One night our family was driving back from Morris, and dad saw a car in the ditch. There were 3 of the town drunks in the car, and they had not been injured but couldn't get the car out of the ditch. Dad put the 3 drunks in our trunk and gave them a ride to town and their homes to sober up. I wonder what would happen today if you stopped and put 3 drunks in your trunk. Probably get sued for something!

Those were carefree days. Every Friday night there was a drawing in downtown Cyrus. Main street was two blocks long. Everyone came to town from the nearby farms, and those of us in town never missed it. They would draw names for prizes from local businessmen at 9:00 p.m. when they blew the fire whistle located on the water tower behind the bank. The whistle was also blown at noon to signal lunch and at 6:00 p.m. to let us kids know it was time to go home for supper. Dinner was at noon, and supper was at night. Lunch was in the forenoon or afternoon.

You never went to anyone's house without being offered food. Our farm friends, the Dosdalls, had a huge dining room table in their big farmhouse. If you asked how many people they could feed at their house the answer was, "As many as there are." Mrs. Dosdall, who we called Auntie Phyllis though she was not a blood relative, was ready to serve dinner or supper once, and another car full of people pulled into the yard. She laughed and either she or my sister Karen said, "Cut the pickles in half! We have more people to feed." I don't recall exactly who said it, but we remembered it and laughed about it often. I remember they had two or three deep freezers in their basement. They had 4 kids; three of them boys who ate well like their father. They were hard working farmers and breakfast was always bacon, eggs and more. I loved staying there overnight especially for the great food. I was good friends with their daughter Carol.

We often went out to their farm during deer hunting season. The men would hunt, and the women would set up a craft table in their dining room and make Christmas decorations. I also recall having fresh venison (deer meat) for dinner at their house the night BEFORE deer hunting season started. You could argue that it was out of the freezer from last season, but those of us in the know knew that it was fresh and somewhere in an outbuilding on one of their farms was a pre-season trophy hanging and cooling. Farmers could feed the deer all fall and be assured of deer in the area the moment hunting season opened. I remember shooting a deer rifle a couple of times in the woods by their house. There was a scoop shovel propped against a tree for a target. Don't know if I hit it or not, but I do remember actually shooting the gun. During pheasant season we kids got more involved. We would run through the fields and scare the pheasants, so they would fly up and be shot in the air.

Once dad sold the farm and moved into Cyrus, when I was a toddler, he kept a small farm about a half mile out of town. He had a concrete block barn on the property, and I remember a corn crib or two (a building with wood sides that were built so air could circulate through and keep the corn dry and avoid mold). We had black Angus beef cattle at the farm. For 4-H projects we had cattle as well as gardens and baking. We would show them at the County Fair in Glenwood (Pope County). One year my sister Karen won Grand Champion and showed her heifer at the State Fair in the Twin Cities. In the winter we would go with dad out to the farm and be sure the cattle's water had not frozen over, plus feed the cows. Newborn calves were fed milk out of a bucket with a nipple out the side of it. We played in the corn crib along with the rats, but it was fun.

Some years dad raised potatoes in the field around the barn along with corn to feed the cattle. After they harvested the potatoes by machine, dad would let the 4-H club, or FFA (Future Farmers of America) club from the high school go behind the potato picker and pick all the potatoes that the machine missed. Then he would pay them per pound for those potatoes. This little farm was on the main highway between Cyrus and Morris, so when the potato harvest was done, we'd sell potatoes by the side of the road in fabric gunny sacks. One old man stopped one day and asked dad if he could have the 100 pound sack of potatoes free if he could lift it with his teeth. Dad said, "Sure," and the guy got the potatoes free!!! I saw it with my own eyes.

I could write an entire book about my dad's sense of humor. It was so much fun to grow up in a happy household.

I'll close this chapter with a letter dad sent me when I was in college. Remember, I was a business major.

*DearPhyllisnov191965willmarminnesotahowareyoubyno
wfineihopewehereatwillmarareawaitingyourarrivaltosp
endthethanksgivingholidayswithusthiswillbefunthego
odpastorsevigwifeandfamilyhavesograciouslyinvitedu
stobetheirguestsonthanksgivingdaysothatwillbealoto
ffunisupposedannywillbecomingwithyouithinkmomisgoi
ngtohavemervinsandgranpaonsundayithinkmaybewewere
goingtherebutthenitwouldbehardforyougalstogetbackin
adecenttimeiamenclosingatenforyousoyouwillhavefundst
ogethomewithihopetohavesomemoreforyounextweeksee
youwednesdaylovedad*

Here are the periods, spaces, capital letters, etc. needed in making this a complete letter . . . .

*QQQWWWEEEERRRTTTYYYUUUIIIOOOPPPAAASSS
DDDFFFGGGHHHJJJKKKLLLIIZZXXCCCVVBBNNNN
MMM,????????*

Spaces:

More Spaces:

*Bye Now,
Dad*

p.s. If you should need more spaces or periods, let me know!!

Chapter 10

The Vagina Monologues

(A Lot About our Daughter's College Years)

Raising a daughter can be daunting. Raising a liberal daughter, with my conservative Norwegian Lutheran background and my husband's background being very similar in philosophy, still surprises me from time to time. When Sonja decided to go to a small Lutheran College in Iowa, I was thrilled. Small church college—must be conservative . . . a nurturing place for my princess. Little did I know that I would probably get more of an education than she.

There aren't many college roommates to talk about. After a couple of unbelievable roommates, we reached deeper in our pockets and paid for private rooms for our daughter's last two years at the college.

We all knew we were in trouble her freshmen year when we arrived early in the morning on the day freshmen could check into their dorms only to find that her roommate and her parents had arrived much earlier, and her parents had "set up shop." They had arranged the furniture, and the mom was putting away her daughter's clothes and dad was setting up the new computer. It didn't appear that they were giving their daughter any say in how or where things were put, and she didn't seem to mind or care. Her father later built a frame above her single bed, and they hung shower-type curtains around it to give her privacy. I wonder if her parents knew that she used it to entertain her boyfriend, in the bed, in privacy, even if our daughter was in the room? Well, there were other issues, but that was the proverbial last straw. The college tries very hard to get roommates to learn to get along, so they don't make it very easy to switch. However, suffice to say that finally they relented, and Sonja moved to a vacant room elsewhere and was lucky enough not to be assigned another roommate for the rest of that freshmen year.

Without going into detail, the second year didn't seem to be any better, and Sonja again moved to another room and again was lucky enough to be alone for the remainder of the year. Sonja had never had to share a room with a sibling, so I'm sure we can't blame her roommates for all of the problems, but these gals did have some weird habits.

Anyway, when signing up for her junior year, we just requested a private room to avoid the hassles of previous years.

If you have never been on a college campus and witnessed move-in day, you have missed quite an experience. The only thing more amazing than how much can be loaded into the family car(s)/pickups/vans/trailers is how much can be fitted into a dorm room. We had been with our son when he first moved into the University of Minnesota in 1998, but it was very low key. The U's dorms were full, and some freshmen, including Erick, were housed in a Days Inn Motel at the edge of campus. They had private baths and maid service weekly. It was like checking into a motel. Erick's subsequent years were spent in a fraternity house, and he lived there year round so we didn't have the annual moving in and out. And because he went to college at the University of Minnesota he didn't have to go far to get anything he forgot at home. Sonja's move-in was quite different. She needed a lot more creature comforts than Erick that is for sure. And Decorah, Iowa, where Luther College is located, is over 100 miles away.

Sonja's 1st year we loaded up our cars early in the morning. We drove two cars. Erick and his wife (girlfriend at that time), my husband and I, and Sonja embarked on the journey. Cars pulled onto the lawn surrounding Sonja's dorm and parked anywhere they wanted to (a tradition that has now been stopped causing parents to haul items a whole lot further). It was kind of comical to watch items being carried across the lawn—computers, refrigerators, lumber to build lofts, tons of Rubbermaid-type bins and baskets, bicycles, chairs, sofas, and an endless amount of laundry baskets, cardboard boxes, and vessels of various sorts bringing everything that students of this decade consider essential for the college experience. After unloading all of the cars, Erick and Amy left to return to Minneapolis, and Joon and I stayed to help Sonja settle in. When I went to college in 1963 I had a couple of suitcases, my trumpet, a portable manual typewriter, and a popcorn popper.

By mid afternoon we were at the local Wal Mart fighting our way up and down the aisles with numerous groups of three (student, mother and father) to get all of the items we forgot and thought she could get along without. Shelving units, storage items, soaps, shampoo, snacks, and candy were flying off the shelves, and in fact, the shelving aisle was plucked like a turkey before Thanksgiving, and employees were bringing in pallets of re-stock as we shopped. The cell phone kiosk had a waiting line as students lined up to get cell service that worked in that area. Move-in day at the college was surely the biggest shopping day of the year at the Decorah Wal Mart followed closely by Parent's Weekend in October because by then the students were settled in enough to figure out a bunch more stuff to hit the parents up for when they arrived. When Joon and I got back in the car and left Sonja at Luther, I was broken hearted. It was a very long and quiet ride back home. We would make the trip many times over the four years she was there. We attended concerts, productions, parent weekends, and finally, graduation.

Vagina Monologues (VM's) . . . . it took me awhile before I could even say the phrase. I joked with my daughter and called them the "magenta" monologues. Well, in her junior year the little dumpling decides to be IN the "magenta" monologues. We drove down to the college for the production. My daughter and I encouraged daddy to spend the evening in the cyber café on campus checking his e-mail and being far enough away from the

VM's so as not to hear what was going on. The production is a compilation of monologues by woman who have something to say about their womanhood. It is a rare experience . . . and at the door they sell chocolate suckers that resemble vaginas, theme t-shirts, etc., and the profits go to charities supporting woman's issues—battered shelters as an example. My daughter's senior year she co-directed the campus' VM production. Still fearing the impact it would make on her dad, we decided that it would again be the one college experience that best be shared by mother and daughter. Rather than drive the 100+ miles alone, I invited my friend Norma, who is also my hairdresser, to ride along and attend the performance. And you thought only the rich and famous travel with their hairdresser! We both enjoyed the day.

The VM production is difficult to explain. You really have to be there. There is humor, yes, lots of humor. There is bad language, yes, lots of bad language. There is sadness, yes, lots of sadness. Excerpts from the lives of women from many walks of life and from many parts of the country/world bring to life real issues that concern and bother woman to this day. The emphasis is on a woman's right to her body. Evidence of this is the yellow plastic tapes across the chairs with black lettering that says "NO RAPE ZONE." An effective object lesson at the end of the production is that they have everyone in the audience stand if they, or someone they know, have been the victim of violence against women. An astonishing number of people rose to their feet. That was probably the most solemn moment of the evening . . . very thought provoking and eye opening for many of us.

So I survived the "magenta" monologues and again am so proud of my daughter and the compassion she shows for all people. She constantly amazes me, and I am always humbled by her compassion for those around her and their circumstances whatever they may be.

When Sonja was in college, we became parents of gay sons even though none of our kids "came out." Sonja has brought home so many friends over the college years, but three gay men stand out as being so close and loved by us that they seem as if they are family. They are Mike and Matt and Allan, and they are pretty special guys who just happen to be gay. I hope we will always keep in touch with them and follow them through life.

When I was growing up the word gay meant happy. Well, it isn't just happy anymore. The stereotypes I grew up with I hope are buried forever. People were called queers, fags and "light in the loafers" to name a few. I don't remember anybody in my small town and smaller high school who ever was able to be openly gay. They were just different and didn't fit in and seemed to leave Cyrus and head for the Twin Cities where I don't know if they "came out" or just disappeared in the crowds. Anyway, I am so glad that the acceptance of gays into society has come as far as it has. There is a ways to go, but at least there is progress.

A few summers ago Sonja suggested I go along with her and some friends to the Gay Pride Parade in downtown Minneapolis. I wasn't at all sure it was someplace I wanted to be, but I figured why not check it out. Well, it was a wonderful, summer, Sunday afternoon, and I had a wonderful time. I've been to a lot of parades in my life, but never had I been with a crowd that was so "family." Nobody shoving and pushing or plunking down in front of me to cut off my view. Everyone was so respectful of one another. People were so friendly I was amazed. The last parade I had gone to in Edina on the 4th of July, I had gone an hour early to get my chair in a good spot for viewing the parade only to have a man come at the last moment and plunk his two children in front of me and let them stand there to watch the parade. I asked him if he could either have his children sit down or move aside so I could see. His reply was, "Parades are for kids." I lost it and was very rude to him reminding him that I had come extra early to get a good seat and didn't think him strolling in at the last minute and taking over was very polite. However, I recall at the Edina parade every year I spent a lot of time asking people to sit down, move over or otherwise let me see the parade. At the Pride parade, I had people ask *me* if I could see, wondered if it was ok to sit in front of me, etc. This was not a one time occurrence. I experienced the same courtesy at every Pride parade I have attended ever since . . . . and I try to go each summer because it is so darn much fun. I don't bother with the Edina parade anymore. Now that my kids are no longer in high school and not in the parade, I don't see any reason to put up with the rude crowd I experienced there year after year. For several years now my favorite 4th of July Parade is in the Minneapolis suburb of Richfield.

A couple of times we have taken the light rail downtown to the parade route. I have a wheelchair I got when I had my knee surgery and have used for years when I want to go somewhere and can't make the distance walking. Or I use it to go to movies so I can sit comfortably rather than squeeze into the theater seats. I call it my "event" chair. Well, the first time we took the light rail, we got on the train, and my daughter wheeled me into the space for wheelchairs, I put on the brakes and sat back to enjoy the ride. Well, my daughter released the right brake when I wasn't paying attention, which is often, and when we hit the first big curve my chair swung out, and I kinda felt like I was back on my favorite ride from childhood, the tilt-a-whirl. We all had a good laugh . . . including most of the other riders on the train.

Another wonderful experience that I was introduced to by Sonja and her "guys" is the Twin Cities Gay Men's Chorus. Not only are they fantastic singers, but their concerts are always so special. I've attended many concerts, and at the first one I attended, I cried at the end when the chorus surrounded the concert hall, and we all joined hands and sang with them "Walk Hand in Hand With Me" which is their signature song.

I think many parents think about what they would do if their son or daughter were gay, much as what they would do if their child got pregnant out of wedlock, or married out of their faith or culture. The most important thing any parent can do if those events occur in life is to just be there, be their parents and give them more support than ever. Is this easier said than done? You bet. But it is so important to always be there for your kids, no matter what.

Sonja was also a good writer. I remember once she wrote about a helicopter landing on a quiet mountaintop and described it down to the smell of the engine fuel in the stillness of the day. She is an avid reader too. She got a gift certificate at Barnes and Nobel from my mom and dad once and went right over and bought *The Complete Works of Shakespeare*. She likes lots of difference books and has a huge collection as she reads some of them over and over. She also loves music and dvd's and has libraries of both of them too. She has introduced me to some books that I have liked (*Twilight*) and some I don't (*Harry Potter*). We enjoy going to movies now and then. She is my daughter, and a dear friend too. We share a lot of inner thoughts which I think is sometimes rare between mothers and daughters.

Chapter 11

The Skinny on Being Fat

(You guessed it—a lot about Life in the Fat Lane)

It is easy to get into the Fat Lane. First, you grow up in an atmosphere where everything that occurs is connected with eating. When I grew up we never went shopping without buying a treat or snack. Every meeting at church seemed to be followed by fellowship, which meant anything from pie and coffee to sandwiches and cake. You never went to anyone's house without being offered lunch. Now I still feel the need to offer people food when they stop in at our house. Food was good, and food was everywhere. I always ate well. I didn't ever sit down and eat a whole container of ice cream or a whole pie like you hear some fat people talk about. I just ate often and ate plenty. I love potatoes, bread, macaroni, and all that white stuff that puts on the pounds. So, I know how I got here, and it is something I have just accepted for my whole life. And, until I started having health-related problems, I didn't try to do much about it.

As long as I can remember, until recent years, buying clothes was always a huge disappointment. As much as I wanted something stylish and "IN," I was stuck to buying what fit and what we could afford. I remember shopping at Lane Bryant in Minneapolis when I was in High School, and we lived

150 miles west of the Twin Cities so the shopping trips were few and far between. For special occasions we often called on a seamstress in our small town of 350 people to make me a dress (i.e. confirmation, prom, etc.). When I was going to go to college, mom and I drove to Minneapolis to shop at Lane Bryant for clothes for college. We didn't wear jeans or slacks to classes when I was at Augsburg College nor when I first went out teaching. I remember how fun it was when we began to wear pants in the workplace, which was well into the 70's . . . at least in small town Minnesota.

When I started to teach out in rural Minnesota in 1967, I sewed almost everything I wore. Double knit fabric was the latest innovation and that stuff wore like iron. My Grandma Felt used to make quilts with the scraps of fabric that me and my sister Karen had after making the double knit frocks, and those quilts are still looking like new in 2009!!

In later years, more and more stores opened for fat girls. My sisters and I called them "fat girls stores," and it was pretty cool to be able to walk in and find all kinds of stuff in our sizes. Although I was the largest of the 3 sisters in our family, we were all "robust" as were both of our parents, our grandparents and a lot of other relatives.

Over the years I got to be a pretty good seamstress, more out of necessity than anything else. However, at some point in time, probably when the kids were older and I had more spare time, I started really enjoying sewing and now sew because it is fun, and saves money, not because I have to. I can pick up any number of catalogs or go on the Internet and find anything I want. Gradually, as the U.S. is getting bigger, I am having a hay day. There are new vendors all the time, catering to the increased girth of the American public. I love it.

Did you know that if a blouse or a shell is too small over your belly, you can take the side seams out under the arms and wear them under bigger blouses or blazers and nobody is any the wiser? This is what you do as you grow out of clothes and don't want to admit it. This is life in the Fat Lane.

So, clothing used to be a problem, but no longer is, except that I have gotten so large now that some styles in the fat girl stores don't come to my size. This, along with not being able to walk or get around without great effort has forced me to do something drastic to lose weight. I joined a Weight Loss Clinic to lose weight and ultimately hope to have gastric bypass surgery to lose more weight. It is not my goal to be skinny, but I am shooting for pleasantly plump.

Did you know that all of the seats in many theaters are not the same size? People living in the Fat Lane do. How do you think the movie goers heads are staggered? Count the seats in each row, and you will find that in some venues, every other row has one more seat. I found this out by accident many years ago. I went to a new theater, and the seat was very comfortable. I went to the same theater awhile later, and the seat was so tight I had black and blue marks on my hips the next day from the metal armrests. I knew I hadn't gained that much weight since the last time I was at that theater so I looked at the seats closely after the movie was done and noticed that some rows seemed to have wider seats than others—every other row. Well, in order to stagger the heads of movie goers, the rows in the middle section had 23 seats in every other row and 24 seats in the opposite rows. And usually the seats on the two sides are angled to create the staggering of the heads and are often the smaller seats. Now, when I go to a theater I simple look at the rows, and if they are staggered, I know that one row will have wider seats than the other, and it is almost always true. This is often true of auditoriums and other types of theaters too. However, as I have reached new heights of weight (you know what I mean) I have started using a wheelchair for movies, graduations, theatre productions, concerts, etc. as I know my butt will fit in MY chair.

When skinny people go out to eat they don't even have to think about what kind of chairs there will be. If there are arms on the chairs they will likely be too tight for me. If they have casters (wheels) I can only get out of the chair if the back of it is against a wall/partition or someone holds the chair while I get out. I haven't fit in a booth for many years. I always have to ask for a table. I often call a new restaurant before going there to find out if their chairs have arms or if they have tables or only booths. It is always a worry when going to a wedding reception or new restaurant because I don't know how far I will have to walk, where I can park, whether I will fit in the chairs or be able to get in on my own. When I walked into a wedding reception in Chicago once and took a look at the small, dainty white folding chairs that surrounded each table in the reception tent, my heart sank. I sat down with the most grace I could muster and barely moved the entire time expecting the chair to scream out in pain and collapse at any time. I would have preferred 2 chairs—one for each "cheek".

I bought an electric wheelchair on Craig's list before our granddaughter was born because she was going to be delivered in a large metropolitan hospital, and I wanted to be sure I could get to see her right away and nobody would have to push my manual wheelchair. A couple of years ago my doctor, at my request, prescribed a walker with a seat on it. My hope was that this would give me added support while walking, plus if I got somewhere and there was no place to sit down and catch my breath, I would have a chair built in. It has and is serving its purpose. I now use it sometimes when I am unsure of accommodations and also to encourage myself to walk more because I know when I poop out I can sit down on my walker anytime.

Of course seating is a problem in transportation too. Planes are a problem. Those rows that have arm rests that can be raised are a godsend for me. Usually I'm traveling with my husband or with kids, so the skinniest person gets to be next to me so I occupy part of their seat. I live in constant fear of being told at the airport that I must buy a second ticket. It is one of many reasons why I don't fly unless under duress. I'm always concerned about safety, of course. Also, I must always ask for a seat belt extender. Did you know they have them on all planes? I also have to get seat belt extenders for our cars, which is why I avoid ever accepting a ride from someone outside of our family because I do not know if I will be able to get into their car nor if the seat belt will go around me.

I can't put my tray down in an airplane because my belly is in the way. My husband is so wonderful. He often pays for me to upgrade to 1st class which has wider seats with more leg room. Meal service is still a problem there too because the trays usually telescope up out of the side armrest and are too close to my belly to put them down level. I have declined meals on plans just because of the inconvenience of the trays. If there is nobody next to me, I use the tray at the empty seat.

Taxi cabs also present a challenge to me, especially in Japan and Korea where the taxis are usually very small, fuel efficient vehicles with not much room for me. I have pressed this protoplasm into some pretty small cabs, and I know that now with the knee problems and arthritis, I would likely not be able to make it into many of them at all. I remember one time when my roommate and I in Korea had to take two cabs home from a shopping location we had gotten to by bus . . . one for her and one for me. These were the little 3-wheeled mini trucks that had our purchases in the back.

Going to the restroom in an airplane has been ok. The only problem is there is no room to get "around" to be able to wipe easily. I have had to wrap the end of my cane with toilet paper and use it as an extension of my arm to wipe in crowded bathrooms. And, of course, on one flight from Minneapolis to L.A. I got a bad case of diarrhea—quite an enjoyable experience.

Going to public bathrooms in Korea and Japan is no picnic. Back in the 70's when I was there, many bathrooms were still holes in the floor over which you would squat to do your business. Fat people don't squat so easily, so I went to great lengths to avoid these types of bathrooms. Of course, when I was young my bladder was a lot more predictable and also a lot stronger. I could shop or sightsee for hours without going to the bathroom so just a little advance planning was all that was needed. I recall with a smile the bathrooms in a beautiful new casino hotel on Busan's white sand beaches that had pictured directions on the back wall of the bathroom stall showing how to use a "western" bathroom. The first instruction was to *turn around.* There were Korean people who told me they thought it really gross that we would sit on the same place as the person(s) using the toilet before us . . . squatting was a lot more hygienic in their opinion. I tend to agree.

On spring break in 1974, I traveled with a couple of teacher friends to Japan. We flew to Osaka and took the bullet train to Tokyo. There was no choice on the train, but to use the

Japanese style bathroom. When I got in the bathroom, I realized that with the moving train (over 100 mph) and the squatting over the hole in the floor, this was going to be a challenge. Add to this that I was wearing a light powder blue double knit pants suit. After assessing the situation I decided to remove my pants and underwear completely and hang them on the hand rail that was obviously there to hang onto while squatting. It took me awhile to arrive at "mission accomplished," but when I returned to my seat I was none the worse for wear. The important thing that I found out later was that they had western toilets on the train—in the other direction!! Who knew??

The only bathroom I have not been able to get into is on a sightseeing bus in Washington, D.C. I didn't know there was any bathroom smaller than those on planes, but the buses have managed to do so. It is a blessing that in most other places there are now handicapped bathrooms. There are 2 places I want to go to but can't because their bathrooms are in the basement. One is a restaurant, and one is a beauty shop I want to try. We have gone to the restaurant, but I have gone to the bathroom immediately before going there, don't drink any beverage while eating, and head home right away or to somewhere that has an accessible bathroom.

I have found that portable potties are great. Always enough room. Just not the most pleasant experience. I recall one particularly cold night and I was at a H.S. football game that my son played in. It was 11 degrees, and there were only about 15 spectators in the whole place. I dressed in many layers and brought along a sleeping back which I pulled over my feet and legs and up to my shoulders to keep me warm. Well, of course I soon had to pee. I left the sleeping bag in the bleachers and limped with my cane to the nearest portable potty. By time I got there, I could barely hold it so pulled down my slacks and sat down very quickly, without looking down. I realized immediately that the cover was DOWN on the potty. Need I say more? I was wet all over. But, I hobbled back to the bleachers, pulled up the sleeping bag to keep warm and watched the rest of the game!!

As I age and naturally need to go to the bathroom more frequently, it only adds to the stress . . . . overweight, bad knees, weak bladder . . . . a walking advertisement for Depends!!

One more thought on going to the bathroom. Imagine when someone of my height and girth and bad knees enters a bathroom where the toilet is so low and so small that it looks like it is for toddlers for potty training. Add to this a ceramic tile floor, a rug with no rubber backing and you can only imagine the difficulty I will be facing when I am done and need to stand up. I usually wear knee hi nylons or socks so in my attempts to stand back up, there is no way to get a good grip. I figured it out once when I was in a friend's bathroom and decided that I would have to call for help or spend the rest of my life in the bathroom, on the pot. Well, I removed my socks, put spit on my fingers and applied it to the bottoms of my feet to create some grip, and I had found the solution. My feet didn't slip and by putting one hand on the wall behind the toilet and one on the wall to the left of me, I was able to rise up and escape the bathroom. Do skinny people ever give this a thought? I think not.

With my bad knees and weight it is difficult to walk, much less exercise. However, over the years I have found a wonderful exercise in water aerobics. Most recently I joined Gold's Gym in Shakopee and have been a regular in the pool for three years. I try to go twice a week, and it is fun. I have always loved the water, and no matter what I look like in a swimming suit I have never avoided the beach or the pool because I enjoy it so much. It likely embarrasses others, but not me!! My husband told me once that it bothers him because he often hears the unkind remarks people make about me. Usually I am out of earshot, or I simply ignore them. I figure it is their problem, not mine.

I've snorkeled in Hawaii, swam in the Atlantic in Miami Beach and been in many, many hotel pools all over the U.S. One time Sonja and I went to a casino hotel for a weekend get-a-way when my husband was out of town, and I forgot my swimming suit. No problem. I wore a black knit tank top and black brief style panty girdle and enjoyed the water as much as ever. The chlorine took the color out of the tank top and the stretch out of the girdle, but I was covered up and doubt that anybody knew it wasn't a swimming suit.

When I started water aerobics I put it in our Christmas letter that year that I was on the Shakopee synchronized swimming team. I do love it, and it has lowered by blood sugar levels, my cholesterol and blood pressure. Last June I started a serious diet and with the help of the swimming and close monitoring of my food intake I have lost almost 50 lbs. so far. My incentive is to lose enough to have a safer gastric by-pass surgery in the near future. Why did it take me 50 years to lose real weight? I got to the point where I felt that if I gained any more weight I would no longer be able to leave the house. Seriously, I had to get to that point before I totally committed myself to losing. I realized that I had gained a lot of weight in the past years. Ten lbs. a year doesn't sound like much, but it sure adds up. I've dieted over the years on many occasions. Once I had lost about 35 or so lbs., I would get lazy and gain it back plus more. I've been on Diet Center, Jenny Craig, Weight Watchers, Atkins, grapefruit and many other diets. None hooked me to continue, so I never really succeeded. I am hopeful that this time will be the real deal and that I will finally get to a manageable weight that will make my older years a lot easier. I want to turn on my blinker and move out of the Fat Lane!!!

Another reason I don't think I've really dedicated myself to losing weight is because I have never thought of myself as fat. In my mind, I have never been fat. I don't know if I was in denial. I think I was just such a positive person that I didn't think my weight prevented me from succeeding in whatever I pursued. I was in high school marching band but had to have my uniform specially altered to fit me. I was in the college concert band—same thing, had to have my dress specially made to fit. I traveled, I applied and got jobs that I wanted, I found a wonderful man who asked me to marry him. I never felt that my weight prevented me from accomplishing my goals. It was even ok when I had my babies. I never looked pregnant until I was quite far along, and I felt great when I was pregnant. I know that it has probably been an embarrassment to my kids to have such a fat mom and my husband to have a fat wife, but somehow as much as I knew intellectually that I should/must lose weight, I just never succeeded. I am so blessed to have been so loved by so many family and friends, in spite of my weight.

I know that there are many fat people who beat themselves up and have low self esteem and blame everything bad that happens to them on the fact that they are fat. I have never done that and probably that is why I have been pretty comfortable with myself for all these years. Until the 1990's my weight was inconvenient. Since then it has begun to take its tole on my health. I developed Type II diabetes and then began gaining more and more weight until now I had to do something about it.

It has been many years since I've shopped at any store that doesn't have an electric shopping cart. They are wonderful—Wal Mart, most every grocery store, Lowe's, Menard's, Target, and others have them by the front door. I notice that most of the riders look a lot like me. It has been wonderful to be able to shop with such ease.

Fat people are cashing in on the baby boomer's generation . . . more attention to the aging population and handicapped individuals has been wonderful for us. I have started going to the State Fair again, after not going for years, because I can rent a cart for the day and enjoy the day like everyone else. I can rent a cart and go to the Renaissance Festival and the Mall of America. These are all venues I love, but for many years didn't go to them until I found out they had the carts.

I've waited at CUB or Wal Mart for up to an hour to get a cart if they are all in use, but it is well worth the wait. I wonder if skinny people ever think about getting to a store or event and not knowing if there will be a way for them to get around and enjoy it? I do.

I went for a recent mammogram and ob/gyn checkup. I love the doctor, but have always hated their waiting room because it is filled with wooden armed chairs that are so snug that if I do sit down in them my hips spread out and when I stand up the chair comes up with me! This last visit, I entered the waiting room and to my surprise they had all new furniture, and there were several "love seat" style seats. I have noticed hospitals and other dentist and doctor offices that have done this, and I'm sure it is to make patients with fat butts more comfortable. Well, when I went into the lab for my mammogram the technician was complaining about the new furniture. She said, "Why do they get those love seat style chairs? Who in the world wants to sit so close to others in the waiting room." I told her that I was so pleased to be able to sit comfortably in the waiting room for the first time ever—and she said, "I had no idea that might be why they have a few of those wider seats." Skinny people don't have a clue of what life is like in the Fat Lane.

I'm not looking for sympathy. Those of us in the Fat Lane should be able to do something about it. It isn't easy, but it is something that can be reversed. Ugly is forever, but fat can be temporary.

Chapter 12

Some Original Poetry

(From My College Years)

1.

Our common ground, our faith in God,
    Brings me close to you.
Our giving of each other
    Shows a love that's true.
Our heartfelt understanding
    Makes our friendship deep.
The joy I have within me,
    I'll forever keep.

I know that I will lose you
    Someday to someone new,
Who'll have that extra something
    I cannot offer you.
Though the greatest joy will not be mine,
    I know that I will be
Ever grateful for the friendship
    You have shown to me!

2.

Look up, what comes what way and how
Who knows the storm, the bending bough.

The rains, the snow, the dark of night
But yet a sun, a light so bright

A cloud, a drop of rain to fall
A speck of light for man and all

A waxen smile, a sterner frown
Places, people, country, town.

The high, the low, the in, the out,
The soft, the loud, the handle, spout

Look up, what comes, what way and how,
Who knows the storm, the bending bough.

3.

Make a joyful noise, bring forth a song,
Praise the Lord, ye earthly throng.

Blaring trumpets, strings and drum
Proclaim your faith to all who come

Just get the beat, a religious swing—
Faith in God's an exciting thing!

4.

I wait for the dawn, the rising sun,
The birds, the dew of a new day begun.

I dare not look back on the struggle of the night,
The tears, the sorrow, the shame

And the suffering I knew would come to an end,
The suffering for which I was to blame.

What good have I done, and who will say,
If my presence on earth was in vain,

For the earthly creature can never know;
The mysteries of Heaven remain!

5.

To look in a mirror is to see yourself
As other people do,
You cannot hide within a mirror,
It stares right back at you.

But a mirror just sees the surface,
A deceiving faulty shell,
It doesn't see the person
That you feel you know so well.

6.

The following was written late at night during final exams:

Ah sleep, what bliss, how nice if I could only be
Lucky enough to indulge in it how much better my eyes
would see.

The circles around my clouded eyes would quickly
disappear
If they were closed in dreamland longer, each night this
time of year.

The pain in my head would cease to be, my aching back
would heal
If silent slumber were only mine, how much better I would
feel.

And yet they tell me, "Phyllis, one third of your life you'll be
Horizontal on a mattress, sleeping blissfully."

Well, I guess Ill have to catch up when I am old and gray
On all that promised slumber for which I've no time
today.

7.

A ray of light, a soft, warm glow
Of friendship never dies,
Unfailing understanding and devotion
In their eyes.

A peace, a calm, their way of life,
No pain, no sorrow now,
They met the foreseen battle,
Their Master showed them how.

8.

Once a day, and sometimes more,
You knock upon my daydream door,
and I say warmly, "Come right in,
I'm glad you're here with me again!"
Then we sit down and have a chat,
Recalling this, discussing that,
Until some task that I must do forces me away from you.

Reluctantly I say good-bye
Smiling with a little sigh,
For though my daydreams bring you near,
I wish that you were really here.
But what reality can't change,
My dreams and wishes can arrange.
And through my wishing you'll be brought,
To me each day, a guest in thought.

9.

And a little lighter one at Christmastime:

When I was just a little girl, my mom, she said to me, "If you act nice
    all year round, you can sit on Santa's knee
And tell him all the things you want to find beneath the tree."

So what did I do, but heed her words, and didn't do no wrong,
And kept on waiting patiently for Santa to come along.

I thought once I heard reindeer hoofs upon our roof at night,
But, gosh, I looked out the window and there weren't a thing in sight.

Then later I heard bells, I really, really did.
But mom and dad didn't believe me cause I was just a kid!!

So, this year I've decided I'll see him, come what may,
He ain't gonna slip right past at night or in the day,

'Cause I got neighbor kids a helpin' in my plan
They're keepin' watch on Christmas Eve and will tell me if they can

See Santa and his reindeer land upon our roof
So if I hear the tapping of a reindeer's dainty hoof,

I'll pull the rope, the one I've got a layin' in my lap,
And the jig'll be up and I'll have Santa in my booby trap!!

10.

And on a much lighter note regarding a house mate at Augsburg:

Guess Who??????

Her hose are filled with runners, her skirts are usually short,
She doesn't wear galoshes, at least on last report.'

She's not extremely graceful and doesn't pretend to be
Of high intelligence quotient like the rest of you—and me.

She really likes to cook and it's surely not in vane,
For once she made some cinders out of plain old sugar cane.

She's ruined a lot of pots and pans, she's filled the house with smoke,

And she'll keep on buying nylons until her pocketbook is broke.

Her jokes are sometimes funny, at least we always laugh,
But we don't always do it just for her behalf.

She even has an alarm clock with a very special dial
That she finally got a 'workin' after many an error and trial.

The greatest thing about her, you really ought to know,
She's a very special girl, and her name is Ellie Moe!

11.

And to my roommate Linda at Christmas:

I tried to find a gift that would suit her fancy best,
Something unique and different never thought of by the rest.

I thought about a wig to put upon her head,
And decided some days later that her hair looked best as red.

I looked at mink lined nighties all done up in gold and red,
But what a waste to buy them and then just go to bed!!

12.

And during a debate on whether to put tinsel on the Christmas tree or not:

A tree without tinsel is a sad thing to see
It doesn't have sparkle and ain't glittery
It doesn't look festive no matter how tall
You see, a tree without tinsel is no tree at all!

13.

'Tis the Season

I go for recorded hymn and carol
I go for holiday apparel
I go for tinseled decoration,
I go for gay illumination.
I go for Christmas card and seal,
I go for charity appeal.
I go for Christmas feast and toddy,
I go for gifts for everybody.

In other words, like other folk
Comes Christmas, and **I go** for broke.

This poem reminded me of a poem I wrote in elementary school. I searched and found the yellowed and dog-eared clipping of the poem, entitled "On Christmas Day." It was published in the local newspaper, *The Cyrus Leader*.

ON CHRISTMAS DAY

On Christmas Day the organ will play,
The audience will sing and a message the preacher will bring.
The Christmas tree is all lit up,
And juice is poured into a cup.
For dinner we will serve fish, (lutefisk)
Some delicious carrots in a dish.

Some people will come here for lunch,
And relatives come for a morning munch.
The gifts we get are all so fine,
Some of them are even mine.

My mother will get a set of dishes,
My dad will get a clock,
And to run my brother's shaver I will get a shock!
My sister will get a doll,
And baby will get a ball.
My brother will get an electric train,
With it he will break the window pane.

Now mom and dad are napping
They are as tired as can be.
Now that Christmas time is here
Hello! To you from me.

Phyllis Tinseth

Chapter 13

I Know a Little About Everything, Just Ask Me

(What You Learn When You Hang Around for 60+ Years)

When I was in college my dad sold his Chevrolet dealership and gas station in Cyrus and they moved to Willmar. He began selling real estate and finally became partners with Irv Severson in Mid State Realty. He learned a lot about the business but didn't much like trying to talk people into buying homes and eventually got into appraising real estate, something he did up until a year before he passed away. I learned a lot about real estate from my dad. He was right along with Joon and I as we bought and sold our first couple of houses. Eventually we went off on our own, but dad always wanted to be included in the discussions, dealings, brain storming, and the like. He almost never left a restaurant without having sketched or brainstormed on the paper napkins or the borders of paper placemats.

We bought our first home in Apple Valley, MN for $36K. As broke as we were this seemed like an outrageous undertaking, but dad showed us the math. With $3K down that he and mom gave us, our actual house payment was a few bucks less than the rent we were paying for a 2-bedroom apartment in

Bloomington, MN that was on the 3ʳᵈ floor of a building without an elevator. When I was pregnant with Jon, Joon would lug the laundry baskets to the basement laundry room before he went to class at Normandale College. Later I would waddle down to the basement, get the baskets out of our locker/storage, along with a book and a lawn chair and spend the morning doing the laundry. When I was done folding the laundry, I would put it back in the basket and put everything back into the storage locker, and Joon would bring it up when he got home from school. When we moved to Apple Valley, Jon was an infant, and laundry brought new challenges. The 3-bedroom rambler had a family room with a bar in the basement, laundry area and storage area. There were fireplaces in the basement and on the main floor. The garage was attached, and there was a lovely yard—on the corner of a cul-de-sac. But no washer or dryer and we had no spare money to buy either one. Well, on the day we did the pre-closing inspection there was a small automatic washing machine in the garage. At the house closing I asked about it, and they said that it didn't work very well so they were leaving it behind. The wife finally confessed to me privately that it worked, but had no bells and whistles and was too small. Joon and a friend hauled it to the basement, plugged it in and it worked just fine. I had no dryer, but there was a clothesline in the back yard for nice days, and we hung lines throughout the storeroom in the basement for other days. Because of Jon's continuing health problems and the long distance from Apple Valley to Children's Hospital in Minneapolis, we sold that first home two years later for the mid $50K's and moved across the river to Bloomington.

While we lived in Apple Valley we had two house guests. My sister quit her teaching job in Clarissa and moved in with us while she looked for a non-teaching job in the Twin Cities. When she found a job at Ebenezer Nursing Home, she moved out into an apartment, then later bought a condo, then a home before marrying and moving to Chicago (Naperville) with her husband, Mike. Another guest we had while living in Apple Valley was a friend of Joon's he had known in Korea and who had moved to Texas. She stayed for awhile and moved back to Texas.

We bought a two story house in Bloomington that had a huge addition on the back with family room and dining room, plus deck. There was a bedroom and bathroom and family room in the basement, plus a bath with shower, and a huge room under the addition that was a rec room. The main floor had 2 bedrooms and a full bath, and a separate living room, and there was a finished 2nd floor with a large room, plus private bedroom. The house had its own well which was used for watering the lawn and doing the laundry. There was a large breezeway between the house and the attached double garage, plus pull-down stairs in the garage leading to a storage loft. The house was perfect for the next year or two because Joon's older brother and his wife and their 3 teenagers and his younger brother and his new bride all immigrated in July and lived with us for quite a few months. Plus, Joon was working for the airline and based in Chicago, so he was only home on Tuesday and Wednesday each week. We had a live-in college student named Pam who babysat days and went to Normandale College in the evenings. And did I mention I was pregnant with Erick? Plus mom moved in with us a week before Erick's due date. Yup, the house was full and busy.

We had a lot of interesting experiences those months. My younger sister-in-law had never seen a dishwasher and spoke almost no English. I found out from Joon that the first meal cleanup shocked her .... we put the dirty dishes into the cupboard without washing them!! Although we had a washer and dryer, the ladies preferred washing the clothes by hand until I had time to teach Washing and Drying 101. Of course they got the hang of it easily. I had to hide clothes that needed to be laundered separately or with certain instructions, or they got thrown in with everything else. I remember especially trying to avoid having good bras and girdles go through the hot cycle in the dryer.

Joon's older brother could figure out and fix almost anything. The disposal froze, he took it apart, I took him to the hardware store, and he rummaged through it until he found what he needed for repairs, and got home and put everything back together and it worked fine. He finished the basement bathroom and shower, worked on our cars when they needed fixing and generally kept busy.

I enrolled their kids in school, went to conferences, helped with homework and suddenly had teenagers in the house. They were great kids, though, so no trouble. Everyone pitched in and helped. We were family' they were not guests. I helped everyone find jobs, learn to drive, learn to ride the bus and generally figure out how to get along in the USA. It was challenging, frustrating at times, but mostly a wonderful experience.

After all of us living under one roof for many months, we began to look for a duplex or double bungalow that we could buy—be close together, but have our own places. We found a lovely double bungalow on Valley View Road in Edina, bought it and moved. The two sides were split level. Joon's older brother and his wife and teenagers lived on the upper two levels of one side with the younger brother and his wife on the lower level. We lived on the other side with Jon and Erick.

This went ok until the dead of winter, and Joon's older brother and wife decided they didn't want to live in Minnesota any longer. Go figure! Anyway, they loaded up everything into a U-Haul truck and moved to Los Angeles. The younger brother and his wife remained on the lower level and we rented the upper two levels to a young couple expecting their first baby. The younger brother and his wife soon followed the others to California.

We didn't much like being landlords, plus Joon's brother needed his equity out of the double bungalow to settle in California. About the time we decided to sell the place, we got a call from the lady and her aunt in California who had sold us the bungalow in the first place. They didn't like California and wanted to move back and wondered if we would be interested in selling the bungalow back to them. We agreed to do so for the same amount we bought it for ($135K), almost exactly a year later to the day. I wonder if they ever figured out how good we did on that deal—we had no realtor to pay, and they offered to have their lawyer take care of the closing and all related costs. We got out of that closing as fast as possible to get the check in the bank before they figured out what happened. They probably didn't care; they were so glad to get their home back, but you never know.

After Joon's brothers left for California, a friend of Joon's came and lived with us a few months while he figured out where to go and what to do with his life. He didn't work, but after sitting around for a few weeks, we decided to put him to work so we had him paint the house gray—it is still gray today. A good friend who was a commercial artist, at Joon's request, drove through the neighborhood and recommended the color for the house. We had met him and his wife, the Bakkens, in Apple Valley and kept friends with them and in touch for many, many years.

Before the closing we found a small story and a half starter home on Abbott Avenue in Edina. We needed someplace quickly, so this was considered an interim move. We got a short term loan from dad so made a cash offer and got the place for $70K. It was a darling little house on a nice corner lot, detached garage with an ally in the back. There was a fireplace, one bathroom, and two bedrooms on the main floor. The 2nd floor was unfinished, but we finished it just in time for a friend of Joon's to come and live for a few months when he split up with his wife.

We began our hunt for a larger house almost immediately and found a house on 70th Street, right across from Cornelia Elementary School. The place was not what we wanted—split level, tuck under garage, busy street, etc. However, the location was fantastic, and the price was great. There were 3 bathrooms, a huge basement family room, and a see-through fireplace between the living room and dining room. While we were living there, Joon's sister YonJa and her son Hyun immigrated to the US. She helped pay for a huge addition to the house—a family room on the main level and a huge bedroom on the lower level. She and her son lived with us for a long time. Another brother of Joon's also immigrated with his wife and son and lived with us for awhile. Their son was the same age as Erick and went to school in Edina until they moved to an apartment in Richfield.

The house on 70th was roomy and except for all of the levels, we loved it there. However, after my dad fell on the stairs a couple of times and my bad knees and weight meant it was tough for me to do all those stairs, we decided it was time to move on. The house had three bathrooms, but none on the main level. So we went house hunting again. You must realize by now that Joon and I love to buy and sell houses and move on. We found a rambler off the busy street, but only a few blocks away so the kids would go to the same elementary school. We moved to Arneson Acres which was a lovely neighborhood just south of 70th street and on the east side of Hwy. 100 on Aspasia Lane. We moved all of our household items on a flatbed trailer owned by a friend/student of Joon's who had a landscaping business. The neighbors probably wondered what kind of people were moving in, not realizing we were only moving a few blocks. Sonja did not want to leave the 70th house. One day I took her back and we walked from room to room and talked about and gathered up all of the good memories from the 70th street house and brought them to Aspasia. It seemed to help. We stayed on Aspasia Lane the longest of any house—all through Erick and Sonja's middle and high school years and until Sonja's last year of college. For us that was a record.

We had one auction in our lives. When we moved to Aspasia we decided to have an auction and buy a lot of new furniture for the move. The Aspasia house also had so many built-ins that we had lots of shelves and units that we would not need there. We sold a lot of stuff and actually had a buyer show up the night before the auction and park in our driveway waiting for the doors to open the next morning. I never thought that was why they were in our driveway so I called the Edina Police, and they made them move out of our driveway and park on the street until morning.

The house on Aspasia Lane was the first time we were "had" in the buying of houses. Once we moved in, problems began to surface that were either covered up or not revealed. The humidifier on the furnace turned out to be a meatloaf pan of water in the housing where a real humidifier once was housed. The first big rainstorm resulted in water flowing in the basement door (it was a walkout basement) and flooding the family room. The window wells also filled with water and seeped into every basement window. We built up dirt around the outside and did other landscaping and solved the problem.

The first time we used the upstairs fireplace, the smoke flooded the living room and styrofoam and debris fell from the chimney into the base. We called a chimney sweep and he found, among other things, a petrified family of raccoons and more styrofoam stuffed in the chimney no doubt to keep out drafts. When we moved in, we turned up the hot water heater from "vacation" to "normal" and the heating up of the water to a real temperature resulted in revealing a leak that spewed steamy hot water all over the laundry room. When we took a bath in the main floor bathroom, water dripped onto the built-in desk in Erick's lower level bedroom from the recessed light fixture above his built-in desk. And, when the furnace ran that fall, there was a noise in the hot air ducts that continued as long as we lived there. We had to use hammers and crow bars to get some of the windows open. At the house closing the lady of the house said they had lived there 11 years and had never used the fireplace, nor had they ever opened any of the windows.

The only good news is that we got the house for $145K in 1994 and sold it in 2004 for over $300K. We found out that the previous owners were in bankruptcy and had no money to make any repairs. That is why we were able to offer so much below their asking price and get the house! When we first looked at the house there was an antique car in the driveway. The man said he was trying to sell it but hadn't been able to do so because it didn't work. A couple of days before the closing we drove by and the car had burned up sitting in the driveway. We always wondered just how that happened?!?!?!?!

We renovated the Aspasia house too. I love contracting and making improvements. There was a screened-in porch on the back of the house. We turned it into a 3-season porch by replacing all of the screens with side-by-side windows, adding a huge bay window, new carpeting, and a new back door. We used it as a dining room, and I used it as a sewing room, plus an office when I was working from home after a surgery. We used a space heater because we did not put in HVAC, but it was usable year round if you were a little bit tough. I loved the room when it was done—nothing but windows overlooking a beautiful treed back yard.

We had long and short term guests at Aspasia Lane also. All of Joon's siblings had immigrated so no more sponsoring of immigrants for us. We had the daughter of Joon's dear friend, Mr. Lee, come and live with us and go to school in Edina during the junior year for her and Sonja who are the same age. The excitement wore off quickly when the realization of the responsibility of hosting JiYeoun set in. She wanted to do everything and go everywhere with Sonja. As much as Sonja enjoyed this, it got old, just as it would if you had a sister following you around. Well JiYeoun soon made friends of her own and began to get into high school life in the U.S. She went to parties, studied hard and got to be a great baker of chocolate chip cookies.

JiYeoun gained quite a few pounds while she stayed with us. I felt bad for that and somewhat responsible . . . after all, I did teach her to bake. She and I got along great. She loved to go shopping and helped around the house when asked. One night she came out of her room (Joon's office was moved out of the 3rd main floor bedroom into the end of the living room while she stayed with us) to ask for help with her homework. She asked, "What is a *llama duke?*" I was stumped so asked her how it was used in a sentence. She said, "After the election, the incumbent president is the *lame duck . . .*" Once I explained it to her, we both had a great laugh. It was a great school year and a lot of extra work to go to more school functions, conferences, and the like, but it was a good experience.

One summer we had two young men as house guests. One was a judo acquaintance Joon had met at many tournaments in Germany, named Peter. The other, who was here at the same time, was Rodrigo, the son of a close friend of Joon's from Brazil. They were about the same age as Erick, so they had some good times. Peter actually went to Bible Camp along with Erick. I never got many details from Erick or Peter, so don't know for sure how the week at camp went. Seems like sons just don't share details with their mom's like daughters do. Anyway, it was a busy time, and I've never cooked so much food in my life. Three teenage boys eat a lot!! And the boy from Brazil was crazy for steak so we grilled often and much!!

Our last move, to date, was from Aspasia Lane in Edina to a one level town home in Shakopee. It was a major down size for us, and we ended up having a local charity bring a huge truck and pick up most everything from the basement and the garage. Our town house has no basement and we no longer have to do the lawn, shovel the snow or do any maintenance or upkeep of the exterior. I have a great main floor laundry room off the kitchen, ane 18' vaulted ceiling in the living room and a huge den across the back that leads out to a patio. The two bedroom suites are totally separated so lots of privacy when Sonja was still living with us. When she moved out we turned her room into a guest bedroom/sewing & craft room/playroom. So now we reside on Boulder Pointe just off Hwy. 169 as it goes south out of Shakopee towards Mankato. My husband thinks its the "boonies," but I love it here. I've joined a local gym and try to go to water aerobics a couple of times a week. I've met some wonderful girlfriends to lunch with, play board games with and laugh with. It is, however, a bit far away from our kids and granddaughter, so we have already been looking at properties closer into the city again. Who knows?

After Joon and I were married and moved to the U.S., he had to study and get his driving permit. Then, he had to learn how to drive. My dad and I both gave behind-the—wheel training and he soon passed his test. Over the years, I gave behind-the-wheel training to many more of Joon's family as they arrived from Korea, as well as our own kids. Erick and Sonja both had had some pre-permit training from my dad. However, it was done without the knowledge of their parents. We found out after they got their licenses. My dad took Erick to the Burnsville Testing site for his driving test, and he spoke with the examiner after the test that Erick scored a 99 on. Dad asked what Erick was docked the point for. The examiner said that Erick's test was flawless, but they don't want the boys to get too cocky, so they never give a perfect 100. Sonja passed her test on the first try too, and they are both very good drivers.

Not all of Joon's family got cars and licenses right away when they moved in with us. Once we found jobs, we had to figure out how to get there. When Erick and Sonja were little, we would take them along, take Joon's sister, or nephew, to the bus station and show them where to get on the bus. Then they would ride the bus to their destination, and we would be there in the car to pick them up because on the weekends the buses didn't run as often, and we didn't want them to have to wait an hour to catch a bus back. It worked. Until they had cars, they used the bus to get to and from work. I knew the ropes on riding the bus because for about a year when we lived on Abbott Ave., I got on the bus on York and commuted back and forth to my office at Housing and Urban Development in downtown Minneapolis. In fact, when Joon's younger brother's wife went into labor I took the bus home at noon because she wanted me with her in the delivery room. That is the only time I was in a delivery room and not the "deliverer." It was pretty cool. However, because of my size, they put me in doctor scrubs. Just another inconvenience in the Fat Lane.

I like to cook and bake. I learned to bake from my mom, but cooking was not something she was very good at. She cooked all meat until it resembled shoe leather, and I remember the first time I ever had a rare roast or steak, as an adult, I was pretty grossed out. Exotic spices to mom were salt and pepper and maybe a bit of paprika in some things. The first time I ever ate pizza I was amazed at how super spicy it was. She made chili with tomato soup—never even used chili powder or any extra spices. Food was very Norwegian at our house. Lots of white and nothing very exotic. Baking, on the other hand, was an art my mom knew well. She made the best donuts in the land; she made rosettes and krumkake along with the best of the ladies in town. Her pies were great; she was known for her angel food cakes (from scratch, there were no cake mixes for angel food when I was young); she made a boiled white frosting that was supposedly the best. However, we were always so excited to go to someone's house where they had actual powdered sugar frosting . . . yum, yum! At Christmas she made thumbprint cookies, spritz, rolled white cookies, and trillbies. For all of my adult life, I have made some or most of these at Christmastime.

It just doesn't seem right not to have these goodies on hand. She always had the freezer full of tins of baked goodies, and I can tell you that me and my sisters ate lots more frozen cookies than she will ever know about. All that baking helped us head for the Fat Lane, but wow was it good.

My mom owned a sewing machine, but sewing was not something she did much of. Mainly she used it to mend and fix seams. I learned to sew in Home Economics class in high school and out of necessity have done a lot of sewing over the years. The old fat lane thing again . . . hard to find clothes big enough and long enough.

My grandma Felt (mom's mom) was the queen of quilting. She made literally hundreds of quilts over her lifetime I am sure. My mom never got interested in quilting, but in the last few years I have taken up the craft. Armed with my Grandma's quilt patterns, and watching some quilters in the early morning on the Home and Garden TV Channel, and reading a couple of books, I've enjoyed making several quilts. I have Grandma's quilting frames in my garage but don't remember exactly how to use them so have had my quilts professionally quilted by machine. I'm also nuts about embroidering. Something I started to do in earnest when I was recovering after surgeries about 10 years ago, and also something I would take along on the plane to distract me from worrying about crashing! So, a couple of my quilts include squares that have embroidery on them that I have done.

Before we knew we were going to move out of our Aspasia house, I got tired of looking at the worn cupboards in the kitchen. I bought a hand sander, a bunch of sand paper, new hardware, and polyurethene and began a huge project refinishing the kitchen cupboards. The kids helped with sanding the highest cupboards and Erick took off all the doors and put them in the garage, so I worked on them out there. It was really a lot of work but also a lot of fun. The tired old cupboards looked like new, and I'm sure when it came time to sell the house, the spiffed up cupboards probably added value.

When we moved to the town house in Shakopee, the kitchen cupboards were new but very plain. No hardware, no trim. Just the kind of thing I love to work on. I made a couple of trips to

Lowe's hardware ('cause they have riding carts for people with poor mobility, like me) and ended up buying hardware, trim for the top of the cupboards and an oak board cut to fit to put across the cupboards on both sides of the kitchen sink in order to pull the look together. I measured, drilled, and installed the hardware. Then, with Sonja's help, we used wood glue to attach the oak spindle trim to the tops of the cupboards. I had sanded them, stained them and poly coated them, so they matched the cupboards exactly. The oak board, which I stained to match, went across from cupboard to cupboard above the sink, and as luck would have it, the trim covered it, so it looks like the shelf across has been there forever and belongs. Pretty fun stuff I think.

In my feeble attempts to learn the Korean language while in Korea, I know I made lots of mistakes. However, my most memorable was when I went to my future husband's family home for the first time to meet his mother, brothers, sisters, etc. I had practiced carefully, so when I left their home I could say goodbye properly. Well, I got nervous, and when we left, I turned to my husband's older brother and in careful Korean told him to "please sit down!"

When I was young we had a pet dog for a short time. One day I was reading the information on the back of the dog food bag and exclaimed to my mom, "It says it is for nursing bitches, mom!" I was totally astonished. I did not know what bitch meant except that it was a bad word I had only heard a time or two and NEVER in our house. She and dad had some good laughs over my youth, my innocence.

Dad loved to play tricks on us kids. Once I was in the bathtub enjoying a soaking bath. I was a teenager at the time. Well, at that time dad smoked cigars. While I was in the tub, he laid down on the floor in the hall and blew cigar smoke under the bathroom door, and when he was sure there was enough smoke so I would see it, he yelled, "FIRE!" I failed to see the humor in this joke as I hopped out of the tub, grabbed a towel and ran out in the hallway only to see dad doubled over with laughter. On another occasion, he put a firecracker under a soup can in the bottom of the stairwell (my bedroom was at the top of the stairwell in a finished second floor of our small house with no walls around it) and lit the match. It woke me!! Once at a wayside rest in Wisconsin our family stopped to eat our picnic lunch packed in the car. They had an old fashioned water pump at the park, and I didn't know how water pumps worked but my dad did. He covered the air intake pipe of the water pump as I pumped and pumped wondering why no water was coming out. When I put my head down by the spout to look closer, he removed his hand and I got totally soaked. We all laughed and enjoyed the fun. At a 4-H Club picnic I was sitting on my knees at the picnic table, and while I was busy talking, he moved a 5 gallon pail of red kool aid in such a way so when I backed off the picnic table seat one foot went directly into the pail. White tennis shoes were popular at that time. So, I was now half popular. The other shoe was pink.

The first car we ever bought for Erick was a black Jeep Wrangler with a light gray hard top. The first thing he wanted was a cloth top to put on in the summer. He admitted that he never liked the gray hard top and wished it was black. Hey, no problem. When he took off the top for the summer and put on the cloth top, I brought my stool out to the garage, sanded down the top and spray painted it black with paint made for metal. Erick loved it, and it made the Wrangler look great. Because I didn't do the proper prep work on the top before painting it, the edges of the black paint would wear off a bit over the long winter, so I just did a quick touch up with the black spray paint each summer. I love to do stuff like that. I think if I were skinny and more mobile I would actually do lots of fun stuff that I'm not able to do.

I have always loved trading cars and have been known to be someone who didn't keep any car very long. This kinda came to an end a few years ago when I bought a minivan that I loved. It was the most comfortable car I had ever had. There was only one flaw . . . it was white. I've never liked white cars, although I've had a couple 'cause the price was right. Anyway, I got tired of the white but not tired of the van and didn't want to trade it off. So, I went to Maaco and had it painted gray. It was like having a brand new car but only cost about $1K, plus they fixed a dent I had incurred while backing into our garage without paying proper attention to the location of the shelf sticking out on the side of the garage. So, I was happy with that van for a couple more years and ended up keeping that car 4-5 years which for me is a record. I've since traded it for another Chrysler mini van which I just traded for a Honda Odyssey. Just when I thought I had the Chrysler for the long term it began to have major problems and out of warranty. The Honda has bumper-to-bumper warranty to 98,000 miles. It will probably outlast me!

I love to organize. I'm not a great housekeeper, the dust gets pretty thick before it bugs me. But, I love to be organized. I have a computer spreadsheet to track books I've read. I have my recipes categorized and in an orderly box. Our Christmas card mailing list is on the computer and tracks who we send cards to and who we receive them from. My home filing system is well organized and updated annually when I do our taxes. I keep my personal phone list on the computer and update it annually and type in all the numbers I've written in since the last update. My cupboards are organized but get out of whack quicker than anything else. I have all of my sewing supplies and notions in bins like the ones used in daycare for cubbies. I have my massive collection of bells (over 200 at last count) categorized by whether they are brass or china or wood or glass; whether they are from a state, or country or destination (like Disneyland) or if they are school bells, Christmas bells or bells with birds on them or bells with flowers on them.

My bell collection, by the way, had a very humble beginning. When Joon first began to travel for Judo he always wanted to bring me something from wherever he went. Well, bells seemed logical, so he began bringing a bell from everywhere he went all over the world. I have cow bells, brass bells, crystal bells, and Lladro bells. I have wooden bells (not great sounding!), tall bells and small bells. I have camel bells, sleigh bells, hand blown glass bells, and a couple of broken bells. I have so many that they can't all be on display, so about 1/3 of my bells are in the buffet, and the rest are in organized and labeled plastic bins in the closet.

One year my mom had to decorate a room at their church in Willmar for the annual Advent Tea. The theme that year was "Ring Those Christmas Bells." I boxed up the 100 or so bells that

I had at the time, and we made a beautiful bell display for the Advent Tea. Another year the theme was "Christmas Around the World." For that year, mom decorated a room in Korean items from our home. We brought dolls and books, vases and knick knacks, lots of decorator items, and a silk screen room divider. Mom even wore my Korean national silk dress to hostess the visitors to the room we had decorated. Lots of fun.

The little town I grew up in did not have a beauty shop. The closest one was 10 miles west in Morris. I always loved to comb and brush my mom and dad's hair when I was young. And, I loved to go with mom to get a perm or haircut. Well, by the time I was 13-14 years old I was a self-proclaimed beautician. I gave haircuts and perms all over town. I gave perms to my mom, grandma, neighbors, and friends. Even a toddler cousin, Barb, got a perm from me. She probably still remembers the tramatic experience. My busiest time of year was Easter, and I actually had to keep a schedule to work everyone in before Easter Sunday.

I gave myself haircuts and perms for years. And, in fact, did so recently just for fun. I gave my daughter a perm once, but her hair is so course and thick that the very weight of the hair pulled the curls almost straight within a week or two. With my kids and husband, my expertise is limited to haircuts. Erick liked me giving him his haircuts, but when he got older he didn't want his friends to know his mom cut his hair. I kept Sonja's hair short, and in my opinion, it was very cute. However, in the 4th or 5th grade she signed herself and me up for a class for moms and daughters to teach moms how to braid hair. Sonja's hair wasn't long enough to braid, but I got the hint. Her hair soon was long enough to braid, and she has kept it long ever since. A couple of years ago she let it grow extra long and we eventually cut off 12". She donated it to Locks of Love. She has done that again recently. Even after the cuts, she was able to get her remaining hair into a pony tail. I covet her thick, beautiful hair.

I think in our 35+ years of marriage, Joon has never had a haircut in a barbershop. My only break from cutting his hair has been when he travels to Korea, and his best friend's mom, Mrs. Lee, who is a beautician, gives him a haircut.

When my kids were young and we were not very affluent, I had a little sideline that I truly enjoyed. My sister, Karen, did lots of catering for weddings. I had fiddled with cake decorating and liked doing it. Well, it wasn't long until I was doing wedding cakes for most of the weddings she catered. I actually was introduced to cake decorating by my aunt Jean from California. She and my uncle Lloyd came back to Minnesota for my Grandma and Grandpa's 40th wedding anniversary in Cyrus. Jean brought along her cake decorating tools and did their anniversary cake. I sat by the table and watched her with great interest. I've never mastered the skill as well as Jean, but she was my inspiration.

I had some interesting experiences with wedding cakes. One couple wanted a carrot cake with cream cheese frosting. It probably tasted great but very hard to work with because of the weight and density of the cake, plus cream cheese in frosting for decorating is harder to work with because it doesn't set up as well as the type of frosting usually used for decorating cakes. It turned out fine and was the largest cake I ever made. It was 42" high when fully assembled on top of the table at the reception hall and was beautiful. It was also my most expensive cake—I think they gave me $300 for it. Wedding cakes are very labor intensive, and in those days I had more time than money so put in lots of sweat equity but probably spent less than $25 for the ingredients for a typical cake.

I made a red velvet cake for my best friend, Iva Dell's, daughter's wedding. I used a pint of red food coloring in the cake!! I did one chocolate wedding cake, which is tough because chocolate cake is more crumbly and hard to work with. One cake, for a military wedding was huge, and had 5 heart shaped extra cakes surrounding it on the table. Pretty impressive. The bride was the daughter of mom and dad's friends, the Slettens.

Heat is a wedding cake's enemy. At one wedding in St. Louis Park it was an especially hot and humid summer afternoon. I delivered and assembled the cake. While waiting for the ceremony to end, the reception hall got extremely warm and had no air conditioning. The trim on the sides of the cake was literally melting and sliding off. I always brought extra tubes of icing to make any repairs of damage that may happen during transport or set up of the cakes. Well, because all of the trim on the sides of this cake were white, I got a butter knife from the kitchen, carefully removed all of the trim, put the icing back into the decorating tubes, and put it in the refrigerator. Just before the reception began, I pulled the icing bags out of the refrigerator and quickly piped a simple trim around the edges. It looked fine. Only I knew what intricate trim had not been put back on the cake.

I did my sister Karen's wedding cake over 10 years ago. It is the last wedding cake I've made. Again, this was on a hot summer day. However, the reception was to be in the party room at my parent's condo, Point of France, in Edina, so I was not concerned about the cake even though Karen and Mike had requested cream cheese in the frosting. However, the air conditioning in that building decided it was working too hard and gave up. Not far into the reception I looked over at the cake in horror. The layers were listing and looked like they would soon just slide off. Karen and Mike quickly went to the cake cutting, so we could avert the pending disaster. If I ever do another wedding cake, I hope it will be in the winter!

One year, while we belonged to Oak Grove Lutheran Church in Richfield, the Sunday School Superintendent asked if I would make a "wedding" style birthday cake for Jesus' birthday celebration they were planning after the annual Sunday School Christmas Program. It was a huge task. Our son, Jon, was about 3-4 years old at the time. After the program everyone congregated in the gymnasium surrounding a huge table with Jesus' birthday cake on it. They began to sing Happy Birthday, and Jon pulled at my sleeve and said, "Mom, tell them they have to wait 'cause Jesus isn't here yet!"

All through school Sonja was very good at volunteering—for her and for me. Probably the most memorable was when she was a flag bearer for the Edina H.S Marching Band. There were several flaggers, and they worked hard to do their routines for marching and for half time shows at football games. Well, they had this great idea to have flags double the size of the normal flags to unfurl during half time at an upcoming football game. Somebody had to make the flags, right? What a challenge that was. We were presented with a bolt of silky flag material, and I think I sewed several miles of seams and hems to make it happen. Well, somebody asked me if I got paid for doing the work. I didn't get cash, but at the half time show when they all unfurled those ginormous (not a word in the 90's) flags, the audience let out a unified "AAAAAHHHH" just like at a fireworks display. It felt pretty darn good to sit there and know that Sonja was participating in it and I had made the flags. Pretty exciting.

Another memorable half time show at EHS was when the parents of the seniors on the football team were introduced. Erick wasn't the star of the team, but we were very proud of his commitment to the team and the wonderful friends he made as a result of being in sports. As each team member was introduced, the parents were asked to walk out to the middle of the field and join their son. I wonder if Erick has any idea how much that meant to me. I am so crazy about football, so proud he was on the team, and so proud to be his mom.

When Erick was younger he made the Edina "traveling team" for basketball. Now remember, I grew up in outstate Minnesota and for years Edina seemed to always win the State Basketball Tournament, and we always cheered for the smaller outstate schools and were anti-Edina . . . . even in the 60's they were called the cake eaters. Not until we lived there did we find out they are no different than any other community. Anyway, when Erick came home from practice one night with his uniform for the traveling basketball team I was awestruck. There hung the familiar Edina green and white uniform that I had never wanted to win. Guess the shoe was now on the other foot for sure. Loved going to his basketball games too.

Sonja played basketball in elementary school for the church team. The teams were coed, and the boys sure didn't give her the ball much. It was still fun to follow her team. She seemed to lose interest and didn't stick with sports beyond elementary school. She put all of her efforts into music and theatre and did very well.

I've learned over the years that most worrying is totally wasted time and effort. On the lighter side, I was worried that Erick and Amy would have a "destination" wedding . . . someplace warm, on a beach, etc. because they had mentioned this when they were first engaged. This presented problems for me. First, I would likely have to fly to the destination. Sometimes flying terrifies me! Next, once there I tried to imagine stumbling on the sandy beach with my cane and sensible shoes. I decided not to say a word. If that was their decision I would just have to deal with it. So, don't worry about it. "Enjoy it no matter how it plays out," I thought. Sometime during their engagement they talked less about a destination and more about a church wedding locally. Good thing I didn't spend any time worrying about that!

My mom worried about something happening to my dad all the time. This was especially bad once they moved to Minneapolis to a condo in Edina. She almost never left home when he was at work or away from their condo because she always wanted to be there when he came home or if he called. Dad used to worry about how she sat home all the time. Interestingly enough, once he passed away any time I would call mom to see if she wanted to go out to eat or go for a drive, she ALWAYS said yes. Back to her worries about dad. Every surgery, every illness (and there were lots of them over the years) worried her so much. When he would go down each morning to swim, she worried that he would drown. I just always felt so much worry from her about dad. In the end, he passed away when his time was done, and all of her worrying was a lot of wasted effort.

I worried about Erick and Sonja going to college, then I worried about them graduating, then I worried about them finding jobs. Good grief. My worrying about those things did not help them in any way. I didn't just worry, I tried to be of assistance in any way I could. If either was late in getting home I wasn't angry as much as I was worried something horrible had happened. I wonder why we all spend so darn much time worrying in this life. It is so unproductive.

After our son died I had to work very hard at not being too overprotective with Erick and Sonja. I suppose I didn't succeed because anyone who has lost a child knows how horrible it is and how hard it is to be realistic about the health and safety of any other children. When Sonja was about 3 years old I began to actually worry (now I'm past worrying into paranoia) that when I left work and would go to pick her up at daycare she wouldn't be there. I decided this was not particularly normal. I also began having what I later learned were "panic attacks." I finally ended up in the emergency room one day with a racing heart beat. They "got the paddles" and zapped me a couple of times. Anyway, they said I should go to my family doctor the next day and I was sent by my Dr. to have an echo cardiogram, and they could find nothing physically wrong with my heart. I looked up a previous family Dr. and went to him for another opinion on what was wrong. He knew our family history and that we had lost Jon to heart defects. He suggested that rather than medicating for panic attacks, I should see a family counselor because there may be other reasons for my panic attacks and racing heart beat.

Joon always knew when I was having an attack during the night. I would awaken with a thump in my chest, then the racing heart beat. Somehow it seemed to help to sit up. I would do deep breathing exercises and relaxation exercises until it calmed down. Anytime he woke up and I was sitting up in bed, he would know what was going on. These went on for years but less and less, thank goodness.

I went to a Christian family counselor for a few months. What all those sessions came down to was that I was blaming myself for Jon's death. I was his mother. I should have been able to save him. I also internalized all my feelings, not letting people know how I really felt about things. Pretty unrealistic stuff. And, the panic attacks are terrifying. You really do feel like you are going to die. Mine would be accompanied by a dizzying moment where I would feel I was going to pass out. It would happen at a kids basketball game, in church, etc. I realized that usually it was when I was in crowds. That is why people who suffer panic attacks often become homebound if they let them get out of control. I remember one particular time when Erick was on the high school Snow Court and we went to the gym for the ceremony where they crowned the Snow King and Queen. Just as Erick was about to walk up the aisle, I had an especially bad attack and thought for sure I would pass out. It is interesting that I never had a panic attack while driving, although I have heard of people who would have to pull off to the side of the road and let them pass. I never told anybody about this until much later. Anyway, gradually they got better and better, and now, I rarely have the attacks and they are much less severe. I have to work at it, though, by relaxing, not getting over anxious and keeping things in perspective. I still worry but keep it from getting out of control.

Before Jon died I started getting migraine headaches. They would worsen and worsen until I would be nauseated and debilitated. Once I threw up, the headache would go away. After he died I never had another migraine. Our bodies really are affected by our emotions and how we deal with them. I have learned not to internalize my feelings so much and "let it out."

Friendships get us through so much in life. I have had many friends over the years, but some are very special. For the past 30 years my best friend has been Iva Dell. We met when I went to work at HUD and became friends. As we got to know each other we found so much in common that bonded us. We can talk for hours and never run out of things to discuss. We have solved many of the world's problems during our chats. There is probably no subject we avoid and nothing we don't feel comfortable sharing with each other. She is always there for me, and I can share my most private thoughts with her and know that she won't judge me and will always keep my confidences. It is a rare thing to have such a friend. I have other good friends who have been with me through the good and the bad. And, if we are separated by miles or years, when we reconnect it is as if we have never been apart.

When our kids were all grown up I recall a conversation with my friend Diana, we talked about friends and that now that our children were out of the nest, we would have to reconnect and actually work at friendships. For so many years our lives were defined by our children and their school and church activities, that we had kinda lost our own identity for awhile. Now we had time for ourselves and needed to make the most of it. Diana has such a wonderful outlook on life and is a very special person. Although we don't get together very often, she and her husband are special people to Joon and me.

As I got older I found that finding new friends was not so easy. To find someone who you connect with takes a bit more effort. One new friend that I found a few years ago was the result of a "pickle spill in aisle 3". I was shopping at CUB. As I rolled down the aisle in the riding cart, a lady in front of me dropped a gallon glass jar of pickles, and it broke in a million pieces. Pickles and pickle juice flew everywhere. I turned around to get out of the way and literally bumped into the cart of a young mom behind me with her little children. We started talking, laughing about the pickles and glad that neither of us were responsible. For some reason we connected, exchanged phone numbers and realized that we lived only a couple of blocks apart. Her husband was a trainer at the gym I belonged too. We became good friends. Because I was retired and she was a stay-at-home mom, we had lots of time to spend together and I got very close to her and her 3 children. She came into my life just after we moved to Shakopee, so I didn't know anybody in town and had started feeling a little lonesome.

My newest friends developed from acquaintances at the water aerobics class at the gym. We got to know each other while flopping around in the pool. There were lots of people in the class, but eventually 4 of us began to create a bond. Two of them are named Nancy. The other is Carol. One Nancy is taller, so I call her big Nancy and the other little Nancy. When big Nancy came to our water aerobics class for the first time, she didn't notice the pegs on the wall for hanging your towel so dropped her towel on the floor next to the pool. When she got in the pool, she turned around and noticed the pegs and commented that she hadn't noticed them. I replied, "I just thought you were a slob." She said she knew right away we would be friends. We both have wicked senses of humor and really enjoy one another's quick wit. Pretty soon we all decided to meet and go out to lunch. Later, we decided to get together for a pot luck at one of our homes and play board games. We have become good friends and now share our lives with one another.

There are so many things you learn in life, from the grandiose to the minute, that would have been nice to know without the "school of hard knocks." Brush your teeth with warm water for instance. Never thought of it, but it is way more comfortable. For years Erick brushed according to our directions and the dentist's—an up and down motion, massage the gums. We forgot one little thing . . . you do the same on the *insides* of the teeth, not just the outsides. Good thing he figured that one out at a young age.

And, make a list . . . every last minute event is a great chance to forget a minor detail. I am the master of lists, but very seldom do I get somewhere or do something and find out a detail has been forgotten. Even Santa makes a list and checks it twice.

We do so many things once—graduate from high school, marry, have kids, get your first job, buy our first house, etc., and what we learn from that one experience doesn't prepare us for much unless we do it again. Sometimes we do things one way and sometimes another. Hard to say which is right and which is wrong. So, we try to pass our experiences on to our friends, to our children, and sometimes to anybody who will listen hoping to help them do it right. Over the years I've tried to pass things on by example, but I know I've done a lot of preaching too, just ask my kids!

Another interesting phenomenon is that the older you get the more you can pull on life experiences to share. It is sometimes hard *not* to come up with a story for almost every subject that comes up in conversation. We all have somebody in our circle of family and friends who has to relate every story, and many of the stories are really of interest only to the person relating the story. They just don't realize it. Maybe that is why I enjoyed writing this book. I didn't bore anybody with my stories because you can quit reading or skip around the pages at will. Yet I could go on and on with story after story and ramble for hours. I guess I wrote this book for me. I just hope some others enjoy it too.

Epilogue

I agonized about what kind of book to write and finally decided to just compile memories. The topics ran together and some things got in chapters that maybe weren't the most appropriate. The biggest problem with a compilation of memories is—how do you finish it? There is no end of memories. You can never really finish. The alternative is to just choose a time and quit. So tonight, sitting at the computer, I've decided to quit. I'm not sure I'm done, and I know I'm not finished, but I quit. It was a fun project. As I delved into my memories, I awakened more and more of them. Finally, I realized that if I didn't quit writing soon, anyone who read the book would know me so well that we'd have no reason to talk.

I left out politics, and I tried to avoid family dynamics. I didn't even touch on some subjects. But I did cover a lot of things that shaped my life and made me who I am. And I am still in the fat lane, but hoping to get out of it soon. For anybody who thought this was just another book about dieting, I'm sorry to disappoint you. This is just about me. And, I happen to be fat.

Get Published, Inc!
Thorofare, NJ 08086
02 September 2009
BA2009245